WEA

-0 : B.1979

6964058

WESTWOOD, J. N.
RAILWAYS OF
INDIA
£4.9!

385.095

HERTFO[

This book is due f
may extend its lo
once only, by pos
the letter and nun
information at the top of this label.

D1587263

)u
or,
rn,
he

RENEWAL
INFORM-

The loan of books in demand cannot be extended.

Please renew/return this item by the last date shown.

So that your telephone call is charged at local rate,
please call the numbers as set out below:

	From Area codes 01923 or 0208:	From the rest of Herts:
Renewals:	01923 471373	01438 737373
Enquiries:	01923 471333	01438 737333
Minicom:	01923 471599	01438 737599

L32b

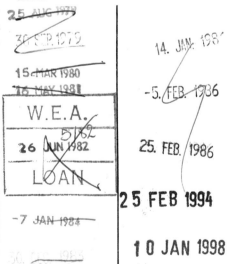

25 AUG 1979

30 SEP 1979

15 MAR 1980

16 MAY 1981

W.E.A.

26 JUN 1982

LOAN

-7 JAN 1984

30 DEC 1983

21. 1. 84

9 MAR 1985

25 JAN 1986

14. JAN. 198

-5. FEB. 1986

25. FEB. 1986

25 FEB 1994

10 JAN 1998

Harrow
10/8/01

2 9 FEB 2008

Essex
3/9/08

9/12

L 33

RAILWAYS OF INDIA

D. & C. books on overseas railways

Hungarian Railways
by P. M. Kalla-Bishop

Italian Railways
by P. M. Kalla-Bishop

Mediterranean Island Railways
by P. M. Kalla-Bishop

Railways of Canada
by Robert F. Legget

Railways of New Zealand
by David B. Leitch

Railways of North Africa
by E. D. Brant

Railways of Rhodesia
by Anthony H. Croxton

Metre Gauge Railways of South and East Switzerland
by John Marshall

RAILWAYS
OF
INDIA

J. N. WESTWOOD

David & Charles : Newton Abbot

London   North Pomfret (VT)   Vancouver

0 7153 6295 X

© J. N. Westwood 1974

All rights reserved. No part of this publication may be repro-
duced, stored in a retrieval system, or transmitted, in any form
or by any means, electronic, mechanical, photocopying,
recording or otherwise, without the prior permission of David
& Charles (Holdings) Limited

3 DEC 1975

HERTFORDSHIRE
COUNTY LIBRARY

385.0954

6964058

Set in 11 on 13pt Pilgrim
and printed in Great Britain
by John Sherratt and Son Limited
for David & Charles (Holdings) Limited
South Devon House Newton Abbot Devon

Published in the United States of America
by David & Charles Inc North Pomfret
Vermont 05053 USA

Published in Canada by Douglas David &
Charles Limited 3645 McKechnie Drive
West Vancouver BC

Contents

List of Illustrations

Except where credited, photographs are by the author

MAPS IN TEXT

CHAPTER ONE

The First Railways

ALTHOUGH India's first main line railways originated in the Railway Mania which gripped British investors in the mid-1840s, it was not until 1853 that the first public line was opened. India was thus a late starter than in Europe and America. Even Russia, which like India was an immense area of great poverty but high potential, ruled through a bureaucracy in a remote capital and needing railways for strategic reasons, had two major trunk lines by 1853.

Part of the reason for India's tardiness was the long drawn-out discussions which preceded the first contracts. Up to 1858, authority in India was divided between the British Government and the East India Company. The latter had lost most of its trading privileges but was still responsible for the government of India; it had its own administrators in India, supervised by its Court of Directors in London. At the same time the British Cabinet, on the advice of its special Board of Control, which advised on India affairs and was headed by a Cabinet Minister, could intervene. Thus to reach agreed decisions was a long process. India's bureaucratic tradition of government, which still persists, with pyramids of committees, reports, minutes, memoranda and instructions preceding any undertaking, has always entailed delay. Under the British, delay was worse because documents travelled greater distances.

Nevertheless before its demise in 1858 the East India Company approved the construction of railways in the Presidencies of Bengal, Bombay and Madras, and in Sind. Of these the first and most important were lines from Bombay (the Great India Peninsula Railway) and from Calcutta (the East Indian Railway). Each could claim to be the first railway in India, although the GIPR ran the first train. These two companies would, it was hoped, build the lines which all agreed should have first priority. The EIR would build from Calcutta westwards over the Ganges plain to Lahore, close to the strategically sensitive North-West frontier, linking en route the military and commercial centres of Patna, Moghal Sarai, Mirzapur, Allahabad, Cawnpore, Agra, Delhi and Ferozepur. The GIPR would link the second great centre of British trade and influence, Bombay, with the Ganges plain, connecting with the EIR. A third company, the Madras Railway, was expected to be the start of what was regarded as the next priority, a link between Madras and Bombay (and thence via the GIPR and EIR to Calcutta).

In 1845, responding to promptings from the railway promoters, the East India Company Court of Directors in London had drawn the attention of the Governor-General in Calcutta to the railway question. The Court considered that there would be substantial freight traffic; but it did not envisage many passengers. It enumerated several obstacles facing railways; floods in the rainy season, winds and hot sun, the depredations of insects and fungi, the unprotected nature of the country traversed and the difficulty of obtaining reliable locomotive men. This catalogue was regarded by some as proof of the Company's opposition to railways; but it is worth pointing out that the problems mentioned did in fact materialise, and that the Company was opposed not so much to railways as to the terms of the contracts which the promoters demanded. The shape of things to come could already be discerned in 1844, when the Provisional Committee of the still unborn EIR Company proposed that the East India Company should guarantee to pay the railway's shareholders a 3 per cent dividend in those years when EIR revenue should prove insufficient. Such a guarantee system was operated by the

French and other Governments to attract investors in railways, and this had proved very satisfactory especially to shareholders.

BIRTH OF THE GUARANTEE SYSTEM

The discussions and arguments which for five years preceded the signing of contracts for India's first railways ended in a triumph for the promoters of the GIPR and of the EIR. It was a triumph especially for the proponents of the EIR, whose skilled manipulation of public opinion set the pattern for future Indian railways and gave shareholders what was virtually a licence to print money. Indeed the Indian railway lobby in its methods and its prize can be best compared with the commercial television lobby in Britain a century later. The terms obtained for investors were such that the flow of British capital for Indian railways became the largest specific flow in nineteenth-century international capital movements.

One difficulty facing the railway promoters was the need to obtain the approval of two institutions at the same time. Approval of the British Parliament (in effect the Cabinet and the Board of Control for Indian affairs) was needed for an Act of Incorporation, while the East India Company signed the contract. The achievement of the EIR's promoters was that by skilful public relations work in India and relentless lobbying in London, they persuaded both authorities first to approve railway construction in India and then to entrust the most important route to their own, rather than to rival, companies. More important for the future, they pressured the East India Company to admit the possibility of guaranteeing a dividend on capital invested and then, step by step, persuaded the unwilling Company to raise this guarantee from the initial 3 per cent to 5 per cent.

The promoters' strength lay largely in the Company's weakness. It had already lost most of its trading privileges and its charter was due for renewal in 1853; it could not afford to lose support in Parliament or in the Cabinet. That its anxiety was not unjustified is evident from, among other things, a letter written by the Governor of Bombay (Falkland, a railway proponent) to a London official in 1849, just as the Company was hesitating over signing the first two railway contracts. Falkland wrote that if the Court of Directors did not give '. . . every necessary guarantee . . . their conduct on this point will be indefensible when the propriety of the renewal of the Charter comes to be discussed.' Unfortunately, too, the Company's record in public works was abysmal; while it had come to favour railways, few had faith in its capacity to build them itself.

In London, the forces ranged on the side of the nascent railway companies were strong. They included banks and shipping companies, which would clearly profit from Indian development; there was Lancashire, eager to tap via the GIPR the raw cotton of the Deccan (especially after 1846, when the failure of the American crop had shown the danger of reliance on a single source); there was the railway and the financial press, ever anxious to extend the range of profitable investments open to its readers. In the press, in Parliament, and at public meetings all kinds of arguments were used by all kinds of people. The economic and 'civilizing' advantages of railways were well aired; there were allusions to Russia, a backward empire whose Government was enthusiastically promoting railways for allegedly strategic reasons. A military committee which had reported unfavourably on the initial proposal for a railway from Bombay was castigated by a gentleman who told a public meeting that Army officers opposed railways because they received expenses as well as pay when they travelled and therefore benefitted from slow transport.

In 1847 all seemed to be going well for the GIPR and the EIR. The Board of Control, feeling the weight of 'public opinion', had agreed to a guarantee of 5 per cent and the 'Honourable Company' (as the East India Company was known) did not seem able to resist. But then there was a series of setbacks. A financial crisis in Britain and revolutions on the Continent of Europe so sapped confidence that the EIR found itself unable to raise the small initial deposit required before signature of contracts. At the same time rival companies were denigrating the EIR's prospects; they suggested that the 5 per cent guarantee meant, at most, an annual payment by the Honourable Company to the railways of a sum equal to 5 per cent of the capital invested. In other words, that the 'guarantee' was no guarantee of a return in years when losses exceeded 5 per cent, because the East India Company was not committed to make good any operating deficits. Hitherto, for some reason, investors had been unaware of this point, and its broaching caused a further loss of confidence. The EIR was compelled to reduce its ambitious construction plan to a small 'experimental' line from Calcutta.

By 1849 the GIPR and EIR were facing dissolution, but at this point a compromise was suggested by the first editor of the *Economist*: the East India Company would be assured that its 5 per cent guarantee meant 5 per cent interest on capital and did not imply any making-up of deficits, while in exchange the GIPR and EIR companies would be assured that they could abandon their stake in the railways at any time, receiving compensation in full. On this basis, in August 1849, the GIPR and EIR signed contracts with the Honourable Company and were immediately granted their Acts of Incorporation.

The substance of the agreements, on which subsequent contracts were patterned, was as follows. The railway companies would raise capital and place it in the hands of the East India Company, drawing out funds as required. Both railway companies would have on their boards an appointee of the East India Company, holding extensive veto powers. For 99 years the Honourable Company guaranteed to advance, in years when the railways' net revenues were insufficient, funds up to the equivalent of 5 per cent of the capital invested. Railway profits were to be devoted in the first instance to meeting the shareholders' expectations of a 5 per cent dividend, thus relieving part or all of the East India Company's guaranteed obligation. Once this 5 per cent had been provided, any remaining profit would be split: half would remain at the disposal of the railway companies and half would go to the Honourable Company in repayment of any interest paid by that company in fulfilment of the guarantee in previous unprofitable years. If the profits were greater than 10 per cent the Honourable Company could require the railways to reduce their charges. Necessary land would be provided free for 99 years by the East India Company, which would approve railway routes, specify standards, and supervise railway operating practices. Mail was to be carried free and troops and Government, including military, stores etc at reduced rates.

Although one clause stated that after 99 years the railways would become the property of the Government of India, with compensation paid only for machinery, buildings and rolling stock, the immediately following clause neatly removed the teeth from this provision: the companies were given the right to hand over their railways to the Government at six months' notice, receiving back all the capital they had expended. In effect, these two clauses meant that the companies could keep their railways for 99 years and then receive partial compensation, or they could keep them for 98 and six months and receive full compensation. In both cases, they would, until the handover, receive up to 5 per cent interest from the Honourable Company (that is, from the Government of India and its taxpayers) in unprofitable years. For the investor this was very much a heads-I-win, tails-you-lose proposition. Moreover, the right of the railways to withdraw gave them great bargaining power; no Government of India could happily face the prospect of taking over railway operations and financing the return of railway capital at six months' notice.

It had been liberal forces like the *Economist*, the Manchester Chamber of Commerce and John Bright whose support had brought the railway companies this prize: a proposition which offered shareholders the possibility of very high profits, a certain 5 per cent interest, and the right to claim back all their money. The ability of the nineteenth century liberal to stand on his head without losing his composure had once more been demonstrated. In 1845 the liberals' vociferous opposition to state regulation of Britain's railways had forced Gladstone to resign from the Board of Trade, but the Indian railway contracts which their pressures had obtained, although they conspicuously maintained the forms of private enterprise, in reality invited investors to put their money not into private enterprise but into a Government guarantee. Moreover, the regulatory powers of the East India Company, exercised through the Government of India, virtually amounted to State control.

All this happened at a time when interest rates in Britain were low, when the Government of India could have obtained railway loans at well below 5 per cent.Within a few years questions would be asked about why the railway promoters were given so good a bargain. The answer seems to be that everyone agreed that India needed railways. There was not much faith in the Honourable Company's ability to build them, and the promoters conducted a skilful compaign. They flatly refused all propositions which did not satisfy them; they influenced public opinion in their favour; and they persuaded all concerned that nobody in his senses would invest money in Indian railways without a substantial guarantee of interest. In reality railways might well have been built without a guarantee; the earliest proposal from Bombay had enthusiastic local support and financial backing, but came to nothing because of an unfavourable report by a military committee. But as soon as the possibility of a guarantee was acknowledged, investors were reluctant to put their money in any unguaranteed enterprise.

Yet there was much to be said in favour of these contracts and the similar contracts which followed. They did succeed in getting railways built, and acquiring for India the latest Western technology. The price paid was unnecessarily high, but the same might be said of other countries' railways. Nevertheless, these first contracts could not be regarded as the final answer, and subsequent Indian transport history revolved around this question of how the railways should be financed, and whether State or private enterprise should build and operate them.

The promoters of the East Indian Railway had dominated the discussions of the late forties. After agreement was reached in 1849 on the terms of the 5 per cent guarantee, surveys were begun for the first section of the line from Calcutta, a section which was regarded as an experimental railway. This line was to run north-westwards to tap the Raniganj coalfield, whose existence had been known from at least the beginning of the century and which, by the end of the century, would be India's main coal producer. Among the proponents of this railway was the P. & O. Steamship Co. which expected great economies if its ships could burn Indian coal in the east, instead of coal transported expensively from Britain. Nevertheless, this first line was never regarded simply as a coal conveyor but rather as the first link of an east to west trunk line.

Calcutta, which remained the capital of India until super-ceded by Delhi in 1912, had a population approaching 500,000 in 1845. It stood 121 miles from the sea on the east bank of the River Hooghly, part of the river system of the Ganges delta. The Hooghly is at its narrowest point at Calcutta, but still 1700ft wide, and there are high and fast tides. This, and the general unpredictability of the Ganges, explain why the EIR chose not to cross the Hooghly into Calcutta. An experimental railway could hardly afford to begin with a long and difficult bridge. Hence the EIR decided to site its eastern terminal at Howrah, on the west bank of the Hooghly opposite Calcutta, and there it remained, although from 1874 the river was crossed at this point by a road bridge.

Surveying took place only in the 'cold weather' (cool season) but the first parcel of land was made available early in 1851 and construction began. The engineering problems were of a kind which became drearily familiar to subsequent generations of railway builders. The greatest were the rivers. Indian rivers have enormously wide beds to accommodate the floods of the rainy season; for the remainder of the year, except for those like the Ganges and Indus which rise among the melting snows of the Himalayas, the rivers are little more than a pathetic trickle, or entirely dry. Thus river bridges must be very long, with piers strong enough to withstand the majestic torrents of the wet season, and with long raised approaches to accommodate waters overflowing the river banks. Sometimes even this is not enough: the rivers from time to time alter their course. More than once, engineers have discovered that the river has shifted before their bridge is finished.

The first experimental section of the EIR had difficulties enough, crossing part of the Ganges delta. The severe flooding to which it was subject was countered by generous provision of culverts and flood arches (a total of 6,700 yards in the 121 miles), of bridges (1,000 yards), and of embankments of wide cross sections and gentle slope. The River Damodar was a special menace, for it burst its banks every year. Like many other Indian rivers its banks were above the level of the surrounding land. The railway builders accordingly removed the raised right bank, ensuring that when the waters rose they would spill only on the side away from the line.

Technical standards set by the EIR would obviously be of great importance to the future of Indian railways, and it was fortunate that at this time the influential voices belonged to men of foresight and experience. Dalhousie, Governor-General of India in 1848–56, had headed the Railway Department of the British Board of Trade in 1845–46 and, like Gladstone, had tried with only limited success to impose a measure of sanity on British railway promoters. Dalhousie was well aware of the need to plan railway routes rather than allow them to be decided chaotically by that interplay of self-interested forces which in Britain had produced, out of the Railway Mania, wasted capital and unnecessary lines. He was also well aware of the need for a standard gauge for all Indian railways, and in this he was supported by Simms, the consulting engineer of the Indian administration. In the 1849 agreements the question of gauge had not even been raised. The East India Company preferred 4ft 8½in, but left the final decision to the Indian administration. Dalhousie preferred 6ft; he had no strong feeling about this, but insisted that whatever gauge was chosen must be regarded as the standard gauge for all India. Simms recommended 5ft 6in. This was a compromise between opposing views, but Simms certainly favoured a broader rather than a narrower gauge. He mentioned recent severe storms whose winds, he said, might well have overturned a narrow-gauge train but could not overcome the extra stability of broad-gauge vehicles. The East India Company Court of Directors thereupon accepted the 5ft 6in gauge. Dalhousie was content, believing that there would only be one gauge in India. When he left in 1856 he had no reason to suspect that within seven years another gauge would be introduced and that India would be plagued with the same gauge problems that beset other British territories.

Simms seems to have had a hand in ensuring standardisation of other dimensions. He also decided that the single-track EIR should have bridges and brickwork which would not require reconstruction should the track be doubled subsequently. This practice was later followed by other railways. Simms left in 1850, being succeeded for a year by Kennedy, a military engineer whose imaginative thinking was often spoiled by his exaggerated talk and careless research. Kennedy was largely responsible for the change of route adopted for the second stage of the EIR. It had been intended to continue the experimental line in due course through its initial terminus at Raniganj directly north-west towards Benares. However, Kennedy and others emphasised the advantages of following the Hooghly northwards, joining the Ganges near Rajmahal (about 190 miles north of Calcutta) and then turning with the Ganges towards the west, following the southern bank of that river. This choice of route was nearly 200 miles longer than the direct route which was already being surveyed, but it had the advantage of passing through the heavily populated Gangetic plain with its large commercial centres. Moreover,

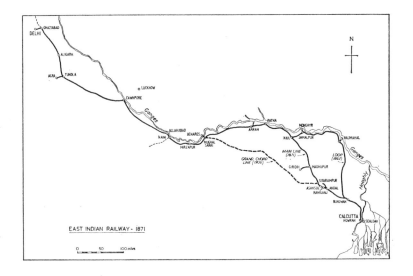

EAST INDIAN RAILWAY - 1871

Rajmahal was the lowest point to which the Ganges was reliably navigable all the year round. The proposed direct route parallel to the Grand Trunk Road was less liable to flooding but passed through desolate tiger-infested terrain. The choice of the longer route meant that Raniganj would remain a branch-line station until 1871, when the so-called 'main line' was completed to join the longer route at Kiul Junction. The second stage of the EIR therefore began not from Raniganj, but from a junction near Burdwan, 67 miles north-west of Calcutta: the future route was fixed from Howrah to Burdwan with a 36-mile branch to the Raniganj coalfield, and from Burdwan to the Ganges and then via Patna, Mirzapur and Allahabad to Delhi (1130 miles). The contract for the extension of the railway to Delhi was signed in 1854, before the opening of the 121-mile line which had been originally sanctioned as an experiment. Meanwhile the railway had indeed proved itself, for the initial section from Howrah to Hooghly (24 miles) began operation in 1854. The London *Times* reprinted an article, 'The First Trot of our Iron Horse', from

the local *Bengal Hurkaru*, written to mark the official first
run:

> On Wednesday *Rawrah* gave the first small earnest of her future
> attractions and greatness. On the day before the locomotive was
> fairly set up it got up steam and astonished the weak minds of
> the suburban inhabitants with its snort and its whistle and its
> fiery speed . . . It was erroneously announced in one of the Calcutta
> newspapers that the start would be made at 1 o'clock in the after-
> noon. At that hour, therefore, the railway terminus at Howrah
> was thronged with spectators from this side of the river . . . It
> appeared that the locomotive had already started . . . and was
> expected to return at 1. But as the hour of 3 drew near many
> were the conjectures why it did not return . . . An up-country
> native whom we overheard made about the shrewdest guess of
> them all—namely, that the delay had arisen owing to the *sahib log*
> in the chariot of fire being engaged in *pet ka peojo*—worship of the
> belly god. This, it appears, was really the case, the party . . .
> having tarried on their way back for refreshments. At length,
> however, when expectation seemed to be at its utmost strain . . .
> the distant and indistinct "snorting" of the iron steed turned the
> eyes of the multitude . . . It came, it sped on and passed out of
> sight to its halting place, ere the assembled crowds could give
> expression to their feelings in shouts . . . The locomotive is pro-
> nounced by competent judges to be a "fine one".

In February 1855 the whole 121-mile route was officially
opened, and the next nine years witnessed extensions as far
as Delhi. Jamalpur (282 miles from Calcutta) was chosen as
the site of the EIR locomotive workshop. One reason for this
choice was to ensure that its workers would not be enticed
by the bright lights and vices of a metropolis. In this Jamalpur
proved to be an excellent choice, for it still remains inhospit-
able and godforsaken. Additionally, it was close to Monghyr,
to which is was linked by branch line. Monghyr was one of
the few places on the Ganges which was assured of deepwater
quays immune to shifting of the river's course; and as the
'Birmingham of the East' it was a traditional metal-working
centre with a population which would be suited for railway
work. The workshops were established in 1862, much of the
machinery arriving by river at Monghyr.

The EIR reached Delhi in 1864. The west bank of the River

Jumna near Agra had been attained in 1862, but it was not until 1908 that a bridge over the Jumna at Agra gave the EIR its own direct access to that city. Similarly, it was not until 1887 that the Dufferin Bridge linked the EIR at Moghal Sarai with the city of Benares. In 1867 a branch from Allahabad to Jabalpur was opened, which with the completion of the Indian Midland's Itarsi-Jabalpur line in 1870 provided the long-sought Bombay-Calcutta trunk route.

Meanwhile work continued on what would be known as the 'main line', the shorter route from Calcutta which had been originally planned. This was finished in 1871, connecting Raniganj with the original EIR line at Kiul. Three decades later an even shorter route between Calcutta and the west would be provided by the 'Grand Chord' from Sitarampur (17 miles west of Raniganj) via Gaya to Moghal Sarai.

THE GREAT INDIAN PENINSULA

In 1843 an engineer who had helped to build England's Great Western Railway (G. T. Clark) went to Bombay to study the possibility of a railway from that port over the Western Ghats and into the plateau beyond. His scheme, although popular in Bombay, was rejected by a committee of army officers appointed by the Government. Meanwhile a rival project for a Great Indian Peninsula Railway envisaged a line up the Western Ghats which would proceed almost due east across the Deccan to the East Coast. From this line branches would go north and south to Allahabad and Madras. Liverpool cotton interests seeking fresh sources of raw cotton, and with an eye on the potential market for cotton goods, supported the project.

Mr Clark and his pressure group soon joined forces with their rivals and eventually a more modest scheme, but still retaining the name Great Indian Peninsula Railway, was proposed. When in 1849 the 5 per cent guarantee was agreed with the East India Company for a 35-mile experimental line, work started almost immediately. The surveys for the first 21-mile section began early in 1850 and were finished within

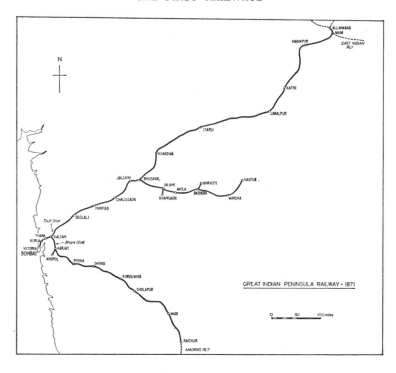

GREAT INDIAN PENINSULA RAILWAY - 1871

a few months. Tenders were invited in September of the same year. In early 1853, Thana, which in 1298 had been described by Marco Polo as a 'great kingdom', once again made history as the destination of what was officially regarded as India's first railway train. This ran on April 16, 1853, honoured by a 21-gun salute but ignored by Falkland, the Governor of Bombay, who preferred to remain in the cool of his hill station. Perhaps the Governor had some excuse, because the 'first train' was no such thing; although in 1953 India celebrated the centenary of her railways, it was in November 1852 that the real first train ran to Thana, conveying directors and their guests. As early as February 1852 the first steam locomotive was pottering around the new GIPR workshops at Byculla (Bombay). This same engine hauled the official 'first' train and was named *Falkland* to honour the Governor. By May 1854 the full 35 miles were open, two tracks running from the east side of Bombay Island, near the docks, to Kalyan at the foot of the Ghats.

Thus by 1855 India's two experimental lines, the GIPR and the EIR, were in operation. Traffic, especially passenger, more than fulfilled expectations. Not for the last time in Indian railway history, more traffic would have been carried if capacity had been available. By mid-1855 about 12,000 third-class passengers and 100 first-class were carried each week. The third class carriages were crammed with standing passengers. Those who had predicted that caste considerations would prevent passengers mingling together in third class compartments and that the Brahmin would never sit down with the Untouchable, were proved wrong. When it was a question of travelling or not travelling, or of the difference between a first-class and third-class ticket, caste was temporarily forgotten.

By this time the GIP was already planning its future extensions, which would take it towards the Ganges and towards Madras by the routes originally envisaged by Clark. Its two spectacular lines over the Western Ghats were complete by 1865, and by 1871 it connected with the Madras Railway in the south east and with the EIR in the centre of the subcontinent, and extended eastwards as far as Nagpur.

OTHER EARLY RAILWAYS

The Government of India, with the approval of the Governor General, Dalhousie, had agreed in 1849 to guarantee a 5 per cent return on the estimated £1m required by the EIR for its experimental line, and on the estimated £500,000 for the GIP Bombay-Kalyan line. At this time these guarantees were not regarded as precedents. Not until 1853 did Dalhousie in a long minute record his views for the future. The general problem was, and would remain, that the Government wanted railways built in India. This was not simply for strategic reasons or for better exploitation of Indian resources. There was also the genuine desire to benefit the population, and at this period the old ideal of non-interference in local life was being replaced by the urge to offer Indians the advantages of Western civilisation. While the government of India wanted railways, however, it lacked the money to build them. Dalhousie himself was exceptional in that he was in at least two minds about the relations between railways and Governments. On the one hand, like so many of his contemporaries, he saw the virtues of private enterprise, especially in India where, he felt, the people had come to believe that if anything needed to be done it would be the restless and innovating British who would do it. On the other hand, in London a decade earlier Dalhousie had been one of the very few voices advocating stricter Government control of railway construction in the United Kingdom.

Dalhousie's celebrated Minute to the East India Company Court of Directors which did so much to shape the evolution of Indian railways, suggested a solution which would combine the benefits of State control with private enterprise. Private companies should be entrusted with railway building and operation, but with their activities closely controlled by the Indian Administration. Dalhousie admitted that the Administration's own engineers would probably be equally competent, but these engineers could hardly be spared from their other tasks. Moreover, the infusion of British enterprise and British capital would probably prove contagious, as they had in France, awakening local initiative and attracting local capital. The companies would accept Government control because they would be well remunerated. The guarantee system would be continued.

Dalhousie's reputation and the knowledge that French railways built under a guarantee system were paying their shareholders about three times more in dividends than the competitive and unguaranteed railways of Britain, were sufficient reason for the acceptance of his Minute, which was adopted in 1854 as the basis of future construction. After a few years it was realised that the contracts based on the Minute were over-generous to the companies, but such contracts did induce eight companies between 1854 and 1860 to start, or continue, lines which included railways which would later form India's trunk routes.

The substance of these contracts was that the railway companies would raise the capital and organise the construction and operation of certain approved lines. The Government (before 1858 the East India Company, after 1858 the Secretary of State for India) would award the contracts and would provide free land for the railways as well as guarantee interest on the capital (this varied from 4½ to 5 per cent according to prevailing rates). In return, the companies submitted to very close Government supervision. In theory the Government had the right to intervene in any matter except the selection of staff, and it was to have a Director with strong powers of veto on the board of each company in London. In practice, the Government approved or specified the routes, set standards of construction which were checked by Government engineers, approved the amount and type of rolling stock, approved passenger and freight tariffs, determined train services, supervised expenditure and maintenance standards, and checked the accounts and specified how they should be presented. Mails were to be carried free, and Government supplies and troops at reduced rates.

In years when profits permitted dividends greater than the dividends guaranteed by the Government, half the surplus was to be paid to the Government in repayment of its earlier disbursements of guaranteed interest in unprofitable years. The companies were to hold their railways on 99-year leases, after which the Government would take them over with fair compensation for plant, equipment and rolling stock. The Government could also take them over after 25 or 50 years on terms reflecting the value of the lines as well as the equipment. For their part, the companies had the right at six months' notice to surrender their lines to the Government in exchange for the capital they had invested. Thus in most respects the pattern of the earlier 1849 contracts was maintained. By the 1860s it was clear that it would have been cheaper for the Government to have built the railways itself, but in fairness to Dalhousie it should be stressed that he had never denied this.

With dividends guaranteed, there was no desire on the companies' part for any great economies in construction. On balance this was not as disastrous as it might have been. It is true that the average cost per mile of line was £18,000 by 1868, whereas Dalhousie had assumed £8,000. Supervision by Government engineers, however, meant that frivolities, extravagances, and gross wastages were checked, while the company engineers were not prevented by financial limitations from building their lines to high technical standards. These standards were often higher than the age demanded, but proved a good investment in later decades.

By the end of 1868, stimulated by the guarantee terms suggested by Dalhousie, Indian railway companies had laid 4,000 miles of track and were surveying or building an additional 2,000. Of the 1868 mileage the GIPR and EIR accounted for 875 and 1,350 respectively. Third place was held by the Madras Railway (678 miles). The Sind Punjab & Delhi Railway had already built 400 miles and the Bombay Baroda and Central India 300. The Eastern Bengal Railway had 114 miles of line, while the Great Southern of India had 168. The remaining mileage consisted of isolated short lines.

The Madras Railway was of the same vintage as the GIPR and EIR but had been less fortunate. It had its origin in 1845, but did not obtain authorisation for its first line until 1853. In the intervening years, however, some valuable surveying had been done by military engineers. It was suggested that the Government should build the railway, and the East India Company agreed. However, the Cabinet's Board of Control insisted on private enterprise. In 1871 the Madras Railway effected a junction with the GIPR at Raichur, having built a 374-mile main line. This route from Madras to Bombay via Raichur was preferred to one via Bangalore because the latter city stood 3,000ft above sea level.

The Madras new terminus near the sea-front at Rayapuram

also accommodated the trains of its western main line. This was destined to serve the West (Malabar) Coast and by 1868 had progressed beyond Salem. It already had an important branch from Jalarpet to Bangalore Cantonment (the remaining three miles to Bangalore City were laid only in 1882).

The Sind Punjab & Delhi, later to form the nucleus of the North Western Railway, emerged from the four separate undertakings which (under one management in London) had attempted to provide a combined steamship and railway route up the valley of the Indus from the new port at Karachi. The steamers proved too weak for the Indus currents, so an all-rail project was adopted. The main line crossed the Sind desert and paralleled the Indus up to Multan, then turned NE to Lahore and Amritsar. The easily-graded Multan–Amritsar section was opened in 1865. Meanwhile, it had been decided that the EIR should not be entrusted with the extension of its Calcutta-Delhi line beyond Delhi towards the NW. Instead the Sind & Punjab Railway (later the Sind Punjab & Delhi) was granted a contract to build a 300-mile line from its terminus at Amritsar to a junction with the EIR at Ghaziabad near Delhi. This was completed in 1870, at last making possible the quick movement of troops to the strategically sensitive NW frontier.

When the GIPR in 1855 was negotiating for a contract to extend its lines beyond Kalyan over the Ghats, a troublesome thorn in its side was a rival company headed by Kennedy, who had condemned the steep gradients and expense which the GIP route would entail. His own company wanted to build a line from Bombay along the West Coast up to Baroda, where it could turn inland to link up with the EIR. Because the coastal strip was flat, Kennedy claimed that his line would be cheap to build and operate. Competition between the two sets of promoters became so fierce that the harassed Governor of Bombay suggested that both railways be offered a guarantee, to which Dalhousie sternly replied: 'Unnecessary and multiplied competition between railway companies has been the bane of that class of enterprise in our own country. The supposed advantage of railway competition to the public, which it seems to serve, has long been perceived to be an utter delusion. I trust that the Government of India will take timely warning. . . .'

However in 1855 Kennedy's company, the Bombay Baroda & Central India Railway, did receive East India Company approval (and guarantee) for a portion of its route, from Surat (136 miles north of Bombay) up the coast north to Baroda, and thence to Ahmedabad. Four years later the BBCIR was authorised to extend its line from Surat to Bombay. It resisted the temptation to join the GIPR at Kalyan so as to run into Bombay on GIP metals, and built its own terminus at Grant Road (the first of several termini which would serve the BBCIR in Bombay; two years later its terminus was two miles closer to the centre, at Churchgate). By 1870 the BBCIR main line from Bombay to Ahmedabad was complete, but its other main broad-gauge route from Baroda to Muttra (for Delhi) was not finished until 1909. Kennedy's costing, as so often was the case with that engineer, proved wildly inaccurate; his route up the coast was certainly flat, but it also crossed several rivers and had flooding and drainage problems. Far from being cheap, it was one of the most expensive of Indian railways.

The cheapest of these early guaranteed railways was the Great Southern of India. Whereas the BBCI cost £20,000 per mile, the GSI laid its line at less than £8000. It traversed prosperous rice-growing lands and its only obstacles were small tributaries and irrigation canals. To avoid flooding, much of its length was built on a 6ft embankment. It opened in 1862, linking the east coast port of Negapatam with the prosperous inland centre of Trichinopoly and then ran on to Erode, where it connected with the Madras Railway. In 1874 the GSI was joined with the Carnatic Railway to form the South Indian Railway.

Two more railways to serve Calcutta were built in the 1860s. The Eastern Bengal Railway had its roots in a disturbance among Indian soldiers due to be shipped across the Bay of Bengal to fight in Burma; a sea voyage implied pollution for the higher caste troops. This led to the building of a road from Dacca into Burma, which in turn focussed attention on the poor communications between Calcutta and Dacca. Calcutta residents promoted the EBR in 1855. The company was incorporated and appointed Brunel as its consulting engineer; his recommendations for this line are among his last work. The railway ran from its elaborate Sealdah terminus in Calcutta northwards along the east bank of the Hooghly, then to Kushtia on the Ganges and to Goalundo.

Steamers, some belonging to the EBR, linked the riverside railheads with Dacca, Assam and elsewhere. The other railway from Calcutta, the Calcutta & South Eastern, tried to raise capital without the incentive of a Government guarantee. Having failed in this, it received a 5 per cent guarantee contract from the Secretary of State for India in 1859. From a terminus adjacent to the EBR at Sealdah it ran south over 30 miles of flat country in the Ganges delta to the site of a new town at Canning on the lower Hooghly. Here it was intended to build a port which, unlike Calcutta, would not be at the mercy of the treacherous Hooghly currents, tides and shoals. The line was started in 1859, and opened in 1862. But the new town was sited below the level of spring tides, the water supply was poor, and the district was unhealthy. A new jetty collapsed. Receipts remained well below operating costs. The directors decided to avail themselves of their contractual right to surrender their line to the Government in exchange for the value of their invested capital. In this way the Calcutta & South Eastern became in 1868 the first Indian railway to be taken over by the Government.

Two other short lines deserve attention because they were the subject of efforts by the Government to have railways built on terms less generous than hitherto. In 1862 20-year subsidies, but not guarantees, were granted to the Indian Branch Railway Company, which planned to build feeder branches in North India, and to the Indian Tramway Company, which built a short branch near Madras. Neither could attract much capital. The Indian Tramway Company was therefore granted a 3 per cent guarantee but went into liquidation, emerging as the Carnatic Railway before being absorbed in the South Indian. The Indian Branch Railway received a 5 per cent guarantee of the usual kind, and changed its name to the Oudh & Rohilkhand Railway to reflect its main preoccupation, the building of lines from Cawnpore to Lucknow and from Moghal Sarai to Lucknow and the North-West.

CONTRACTORS AND CONSTRUCTORS

As soon as they had received their contracts and raised their capital, the railway companies had to organise the construction of their lines. In most cases, they had already decided to whom the construction works should be entrusted. The GIPR and EBR preferred to give large contracts to well-established English firms, whereas the Madras Railway put the main responsibility on its own engineers. The EIR divided its line into sections, each entrusted to a local contractor who was expected to cope better with Indian conditions than an English firm. But many of these EIR contractors found their tasks too big, exhausting their capital reserves before completing the work, or falling badly behind schedule. Attempts to stimulate the laggards by withholding cash advances only led to additional bankruptcies and in the end the EIR's own engineers had to take over many sections; from the start they had been responsible for the major engineering works. Thomas Brassey, the most celebrated of British contractors, had refused the EIR contract in 1853, but in 1858 he obtained the Eastern Bengal Railway contract and built the 112 miles from Calcutta to Kushtia. Because the Government was slow to make land available, and because labour costs were higher than expected, Brassey lost money on the job; but in 1864 he contracted to build the Delhi Railway (the Delhi extension of the Sind & Punjab) for £14,630 a mile. He finished the easternmost section (Ambala–Ghaziabad) two years ahead of schedule but was held up on the other sections by the difficult bridges over the Jumna, Sutlej, and Beas rivers. Finally, Brassey obtained the contract for the 147-mile EIR 'main line', which he began in 1865 and which, because contractors were now offered 'cost plus' agreements, proved very profitable.

As already suggested, the main obstacles facing Indian railway builders were rivers and floods. Some of the more notable bridges are mentioned later, as are the heavily engineered GIPR main lines over the Ghats. These, however, were not the only troubles. In general, railway construction was slower than had been hoped. Apart from the rivers and the Western Ghats, the terrain was usually not difficult. It is true that the EIR 'main line' passed through desolate and hilly country with a troublesome tiger population, but the ruling grade was no worse than 1 in 100. The Madras Railway's SW main line passed through malarial jungle but here again the problems were no greater than those faced by railway builders in other parts of the world. After the insurrection of 1857 (the 'Mutiny') prices and wages rose. This embarrassed many contractors, but labour was never really scarce even though productivity was low. It was usual to hire not individual workers, but families; all except children under ten would be employed, typically on earthworks, using head baskets. In the more desolate areas labour did become scarce, and workers brought in from elsewhere seemed more vulnerable to outbreaks of cholera. Apart from labourers, masons, carpenters, and smiths were available, although at times high wages were necessary to attract enough of them.

As might have been expected, the railways themselves stimulated wage increases. In Bengal in the 1850s masons' wages increased from around sevenpence a day to tenpence or more. British supervisory and artisan staff caused a heavy financial outlay. To attract and to hold them it was necessary to pay them roughly double the wage rates they would receive in Britain, plus generous allowances. Their passages were paid, and they were provided with medical care; this they often needed, for they were hard-working, hard-drinking, and reckless. The turnover of expatriate staff was high, death and incapacitating sickness alone removing 5 per cent of them each year. Except in Madras, where locomotive crew training was available to Indians, there was little success (and little effort) in finding Indian substitutes for expatriates.

Only rarely did hostile populations hold up railway construction. The Mutiny was a special case and delayed the construction of the EIR and the Delhi Railway; other lines were hardly affected, for the insurrection though serious, was localised in the North. The siege of 'the little house at Arrah', which captured Victorian imaginations, was largely a railway affair, for it was engineers building the EIR bridge over the Sone who provided the defences.

In most of India good stone could be found, but the EIR was not well provided. Native-made bricks were of poor quality, so the railway's own engineers shouldered yet another task, the organisation of brickworks. Even so, bricks were short and expensive, and girder bridges were often built where brick arches would have been technically sufficient.

The Madras Railway made great use of Bangalore granite, using this material for sleepers and telegraph poles. Sleepers were a problem for most railways (including the Madras Railway, which soon became dissatisfied with granite). There were plenty of good forests in India, but sleeper production was so slow that it was often quicker to order from Britain. For that reason the Government established its Woods & Forests Department, to supervise planting, conservation and felling. By that time most teak and sal trees growing close to the railway routes had disappeared, and would take 25 years to replace. Various chemical processes were tried in the hope of improving soft jungle timber.

The EIR in the 1850s tried cast-iron sleepers but frequent breakages spoiled this idea. In Madras and Bombay Presidencies pot sleepers were used. White ants proved less of a menace than expected; their earth galleries, which they built as they burrowed, tended to disintegrate when a train passed. On average a wooden sleeper lasted only seven years. Telegraph poles lasted longer than this, except when they were uprooted by elephants; in some areas rings of iron spikes were fitted round the poles as a deterrent.

At this period good-quality iron was produced in India but it was expensive and in short supply. Ironwork and rails were therefore imported from Britain. Where these imports could

Page 33 (above) Bhore Ghat reversing station on the GIPR Bombay–Poona line (now electrified) as it was until 1928, showing the catch siding for runaway trains; (below) an oriental St Pancras: the GIPR Bombay Victoria terminus

Page 34 (above) The South Indian Railway's Madras Egmore Station; (below) Jumna Bridge, Delhi, carrying the main lines to Calcutta and to the North-West

be transported by rail the freight charges were not high, but elsewhere transport was a costly problem. Since railways were often built in sections, many engineering projects were unconnected with the ports except by bullock cart or river. Country boats tended to disappear or run aground; the EIR acquired its own fleet to transport ironwork, but the Ganges remained a slow and unreliable carrier.

On a cost per mile basis the EIR 'main line' was the most expensive at £22,000, but this was double-track. On a single-track basis, the BBCI at £20,000 cost most, followed by the EIR at £17,000. The GSI was exceptionally cheap at £7,700. Compared with those of British railways these costs were low. The London & North Western, for example, cost £62,000 a mile. The Indian railways, apart from low labour costs, had several advantages. They were spared the expensive battles which British companies had to fight to obtain Parliamentary approval. Whereas the Great Western paid out £750,000 for legal and Parliamentary expenses, the GIPR and EIR each spent only about £4000. Moreover, the Indian railways did not need to purchase land; they received it free from the Government. In the Calcutta region this concession must have reduced costs by about £2500 a mile.

A parliamentary select committee of 1858 reported that delays in constructing Indian railways were caused mainly by animosity between engineers, the distances over which supplies and materials had to be transported, failure of contractors, and time-consuming correspondence. Its main recommendation was that a less bureaucratic approach would be well worthwhile, that Government officials should be discouraged from following the strict letter of the regulations but should rather bear in mind the spirit of their duties. This was not the last time that this kind of advice was needed, but for some years after 1858 relations between the Government and railway engineers did become easier. The root of the problem was that by the terms of the contracts the Government of India had detailed control of constructional standards. Having agreed to the 5 per cent guarantee, it took care to ensure that the companies' engineers not only built safely, but also reasonably cheaply. The company engineers were responsible for design, but could not act without the approval of the Government's inspecting engineers. The latter might cause costly delays by referring matters to their Government Secretary. Frequently the company engineers were told to change their plans. Not unnaturally bureaucratic delays and implied criticism were resented, and the company engineers began to withold as much information as possible while the Government engineers, in the best bureaucratic tradition, seized on the most inconsequential matters and, unwilling to accept responsibility themselves, referred them to the Government. Sometimes London was consulted, and this caused even more delay and frustration.

Because of Government supervision the far-sighted Thomas Brassey refused the contract to build the EIR's first line. After 1858, the inspectors relaxed their control, but by 1870 the same kind of complaints were being made again. One engineer had to prepare and send in 14 different plans for one bridge. Engineers were reluctant to mention the estimated price of materials for their works, knowing quite well that whatever figure they quoted they would still be requested to re-examine their 'excessive' costs. On the other hand, Government inspection did play a positive role. Not only did it maintain safety standards but at times protected the native population. Engineers who removed one bank of the River Damodar so that any flooding would be on the side away from the railway might congratulate themselves, but the local inhabitants saw things differently. Some engineers used press-gang methods to obtain workers or tried to force their labourers to work for nothing. In Patna Government officials had to intervene when the EIR engineers provoked disturbances by destroying without compensation buildings which stood in the alignment, and by laying their tracks on holy ground.

THE RESULTS

Except for a few exceptional cases like that of the Calcutta

& South Eastern, traffic fulfilled or more than fulfilled expectations. In 1866 the EIR was operating 15 trains each way
daily. The overwhelming demands for passenger tickets have
already been mentioned. Freight traffic developed more steadily but by 1869 accounted for 66 per cent of the revenue,
compared with 4 per cent in 1853–54. In 1869 16m passengers
and 12m tons of freight were carried. The Eastern Bengal Railway had the densest traffic: 11,000 passengers and 1200 tons
per mile of track in 1869. But in freight receipts per mile the
EIR (£1200) and GIP (£1130) easily surpassed the EBR (£680).
Net revenues of Indian railways rose slowly, from .22 per cent
of expended capital in 1854 to three per cent in 1869. In 1866
all railways except the Calcutta & South Eastern made a profit,
but only the GIPR and EIR were able to reach a 5 per cent
return. Thus the Government was called on to pay large sums
in accordance with the guarantees. By mid-1868 the Government had paid about £23m as interest, but was already receiving repayments from the most profitable lines.

Promoters and advocates of railway building did not give
great prominence to financial rewards, except in their company prospectuses. Usually it was more lofty considerations
which were publicised, such as the economic, social and
'moral' benefits which the railways would bring to the Queen's
loyal Indian subjects. These benefits were indeed real, but
some of the claims and aspirations should be treated with
caution. For example, two-fifths of the capital invested in
Indian railways was spent not in India but in Britain. With
a few notable exceptions it was European local contractors
rather than Indian contractors who were entrusted with that
part of the construction work not given to the large British
firms. Although it was sincerely hoped in official quarters that
Indian capital would be put into the railway companies, in
fact by 1868 of the 50,000 holders of Indian railway shares,
only 400 were Indians; there would have been more if it had
been made possible to transfer such shares in India as well as
in London.

Sir Charles Trevelyan, who during this period had served as

Finance Member of the Government of India, told the Society of Arts in 1870 that the railway had emancipated the *Ryots* (peasants) and their families from the village moneylender and brought enrichment. He spoke of ryots being 'elevated to a state of physical ease and abundance'. Undoubtedly the railways did improve their situation. The village moneylender was also the village grain dealer; when the railways came the peasants were no longer forced to sell their grain to him at the price he set, but could seek out buyers further afield. In this way the ryot had an improved bargaining position, made more money and paid more tax (out of which, of course, the Government paid its annual guaranteed interest to railway shareholders). Also, the peasants were the largest element in those millions of poorer people who availed themselves of cheap railway travel to move around the country, seeing their relatives, looking for jobs or visiting previously inaccessible holy places.

The uplifting capacity of railways was also emphasised by Davidson, in his *The Railways of India* (1868): 'There is a hope that, combined with the prosperity wealth and civilisation which have been created and fostered by the railways of India, the blesings also of a spiritual Christianity, based on the truth of God's word, may ere long spread extensively over the length and breadth of that land, which has for so many ages remained covered with the pall of apathy and vice that false religions of every kind invariably throw over the countries in which they exist.' Davidson's sentiments were not at all unique; writers on Indian railways included such perorations almost as a matter of duty. It is well to accept them as a reminder that there was indeed a connection between railways and Western civilisation. Nor was it entirely by accident that the coming of the railways coincided with a deterioration of relationships between the British and Indians.

At the beginning of the century the British in India had been little interested in changing the local culture, or even of extending their own dominions beyond the Presidencies of Calcutta, Bombay, and Madras. But by the time Dalhousie arrived there were new pressures which the Governor General soon expressed in policies. Dalhousie, given a pretext, would annex formerly independent princely States, and he offered to Indians an alternative to their own culture. This alternative included, notably, English-style education, postal and telegraph services, and railways. Indians were not required to accept and use these innovations, but many did. All, especially schools and railways, were implicitly opposed to traditional culture which meant traditional religion because Hinduism was not a Sundays-only formality but a whole way of life. Into this changed climate came the evangelisers, who implied that the benefits of western civilisation were inseparable from worship of the western god; if Indians wanted railways they would have to have god as well. Thus to fervent Hindus the railways were associated with an attack on their souls. It was not just a question of gods; the very nature of the railway, demanding punctuality and exactitude, breaking down caste, was also alien. The railways, despite their attractions, could only be regarded by Hindus as an important component of the apparent British threat to their religion and culture. As such, the railways must be regarded as partly responsible for the 1857 Indian Mutiny, which was largely a popular reaction against western-style modernisation.

The Mutiny accelerated a trend towards less easy relationships between Europeans and Indians, and towards a mildly racialist attitude on the part of many British. Before the railway age most Britons in India, being sure of their own quality, were able to mix freely and equally with those Indians, whom they found congenial. With the railways and other developments came another, less assured, type of Briton who, with the increase in the number of British wives in India, swung the British communities there into a more exclusive way of life. There developed a patronising, often contemptuous attitude towards Indians, and because it was on the railways that Indians and Britons came into frequent contact, cases of offence were often given. Skilled workers from England, or ex-soldiers of the Indian army who joined the railway service, were not the kind of people who would let slip opportunities of asserting their national or racial superiority. At times the Government inspectors intervened. For example, the Under-Secretary of the Public Works Department wrote to the Bengal Government's railway branch in 1865:

> I am directed to bring to the notice of the Lieutenant Governor that, at a station near Bhaugulpur, a Native gentleman was not long since hurried out of a carriage, and not allowed to get out his property, which was thrown out and scattered . . . I am to desire that it may be impressed upon the Consulting Engineer and his Deputies that the Governor General in Council looks to them to ensure the removal of these causes of complaint, which are alike injurious to the Railway Company and discreditable to its officers, and, indeed to the British character generally.

Government officials' dislike of the attitude of some of their fellow-countrymen towards Indians was genuine, but in practice officials were also tending to lose contact with Indian life. Here again the railways were partly to blame. Whenever a new mode of transport is developed it is customary to expatiate on the closer contacts and understanding it will bring between different people or communities. Probably the steamship was the last innovation which justified such claims. Faster travel implies not more, but less, contact. In his auto-biographical *Forty One Years in India*, Lord Roberts recounts how as a young subaltern he went from Calcutta to join his regiment at Peshawar on the NW frontier. The first month he spent in a barge being towed to Benares by a steamer. From Benares he went by horse-drawn conveyance to Meerut, and for the rest of the journey sat in a palanquin. The entire trip took three months. Government officials travelled in the same way until the railways made it possible to rush from Calcutta to Peshawar in a reserved first class compartment, equipped with shower, toilet, sleeping berths and a table to which European-style meals were brought. It is not hard to judge which of these two modes of travel led to better knowledge of India and Indians.

The railways certainly united India, and for this reason they were resented by many. Unification is all too often a euphemism for centralisation, for the subordination of local institutions, and this was especially true in India with its many peoples and its local loyalties. But the foregoing is not intended to deny the benefits which the railways brought to India, but rather to point out that some had cause to regard those benefits as negative. In a House of Lords debate on Indian railways in 1850 one speaker drew the attention of his peers to the relics left behind 'by great Hindoo Governors' and suggested that the time had come 'for England to step forward and lay down for herself some lasting memorials which might tell the future ages that amidst all her triumphs and glories she did not neglect her duty to her subjects.' To suggest that Queen Victoria's railways should compete with Shah Jehan's Taj Mahal was perhaps eccentric, but nevertheless not without percipience. A century later, when independent India began to build its own memorials for the future, the foundations included the well-built railway system which it had inherited from the British.

CHAPTER TWO

Railways of Imperial India

THE GAUGE PROBLEM

THE year 1868 may be regarded as the last year of the first period of Indian railway building, because for several years from 1869 the Government avoided the guarantee system, apart from some extensions to already existing companies; in general, during these years it was the State that built new lines. But from about 1880 modified guarantee terms came into favour, as it was realised that the rate of construction by the State alone was insufficient for India's needs. Meanwhile, and right up to independence in 1947, the State was acquiring piecemeal the major privately owned systems.

In 1868 there were 4000 route miles open for traffic. This grew to 43,000 miles in 1937, before the separation of the Burma Railways from Indian administration and the lifting of branch lines during World War II brought the mileage down to 40,500 on the eve of independence and the partition of the former Indian Empire into the Dominions (now Republics) of India and Pakistan. Of those 40,500 miles in 1947, the 5ft 6in gauge accounted for half. The metre gauge route mileage totalled 16,000 miles, and narrower gauges 4000. Dalhousie's dream of a single standard gauge remained a dream, although ever since the introduction of the metre gauge it had been realised that a gauge problem was being created.

Before introduction of the metre gauge, two branch lines were constructed on gauges narrower than 5ft 6in, but they were regarded as only temporary standards, to be upgraded when financial circumstances permitted. The metre gauge had its origins in the decision that the Government itself should build future railways. This decision brought the Government face to face with the problem of railway finance, and since funds were never sufficient, the expedient of a narrower and therefore cheaper gauge seemed acceptable. The advocates of a narrower gauge could point out that the existing broad-gauge railways on average still represented a financial burden, that there was still a great need for railway construction, and that therefore a cheaper standard of railway was unavoidable. Successful narrow-gauge railways elsewhere in the world, such as the Festiniog Railway with its Fairlie locomotives, were quoted as examples which a wise Indian Government should imitate. The choice for India it was urged, was not between broad and narrow gauge, but between a narrow gauge and no new railways at all.

The possibility of a narrow gauge seems to have been raised officially for the first time in 1868, when the Viceroy (Lawrence) wrote that it would be wrong to reject narrow-gauge railways. The Administration replied that short narrow-gauge lines were not such a good idea as some people believed, because, to justify the extra cost of transhipping from a narrow-gauge feeder line to the broad-gauge trunk line, the narrow-gauge line would have to carry its goods over a worthwhile distance. The next Viceroy (Mayo) made the metre gauge a reality.

In 1851 Dalhousie had written: 'The British Legislature fell into mischievous error permitting the introduction of two gauges in the United Kingdom . . . The Government of India has in its power, and no doubt will carefully provide that, however widely the railway system may be extended in this Empire in the time to come, these great evils should be averted . . .' Mayo had another opinion on the gauge question, being quoted as saying: 'When we have an elephant's load, we may use an elephant, but when we have only a donkey's load, we have to use a donkey.' A committee was set up to study the question in 1870, and Mayo engaged an American engineer to advise him. It was decided that less productive areas such as Rajputana and the Punjab should be opened up by metre-gauge railways, which would be more suited than the broad gauge to handle the limited traffic expected. Mayo himself decided which of the narow gauges should be adopted. Narrow-gauge enthusiasts were divided between supporters of a 3ft 6in gauge, which had been chosen for lines in other British territories, and 2ft 9in, which was cheaper and quite adequate for the expected traffic. Mayo rejected 2ft 9in because this gauge was untried elsewhere, and because cavalry horses could not travel two abreast on a 2ft 9in gauge vehicle. He compromised by favouring 3ft 3in. But as he was at that time planning to introduce the metric system into India, he decided that metre gauge was preferable. Hence the 3ft 3⅜in choice; but 80 more years were to pass before the metric system was introduced generally.

A 'battle of the gauges' began almost immediately. Some of the railways intended to be built on the metre gauge had a strategic significance, especially the Indus valley and Peshawar lines. The Comander-in-Chief objected that this would mean time-consuming transhipment of troops and stores en route to any possible emergency on the NW frontier. Later he agreed that a metre-gauge line was better, from the military point of view, than no line at all. When objections were raised, however, in the House of Commons to this gauge policy, the C-in-C reverted to his original opposition and demanded broad-gauge tracks for these lines. Finally, after Gladstone's Cabinet resigned in 1874, the Secretary of State for India (Lord Salisbury) stipulated a broad gauge, and those sections which had already been completed to the metre gauge were taken up and relaid. But this was only a minor setback for the metre gauge lobby, and when in 1879 the Government of India confirmed that the Rajputana–Malwa line should be metre-gauge, the status of that gauge was assured, for this line was an immediate success.When it opened it expected to run one train each way daily, but discovered that six pairs were needed. By the turn of the century it had grown to 1670 miles and provided a through route between Delhi, Agra and Ahmedabad. Since it was worked by the BBCIR, which already had a broad-gauge line from Bombay to Ahmedabad, it provided an alternative route between Bombay and Delhi. It commonly returned 10 per cent on capital.

The reversion to private railway construction in the 1880s occasioned more engagements in the gauge war. It was feared that the metre gauge, originally adopted as a cheap way of building secondary lines, would evolve into a network rivalling and competing with the broad-gauge railways. In 1884 a Select Committee of the House of Commons confirmed the correctness of the Government of India policy of metre gauge for local and secondary lines only, adding that feeder branches to the broad gauge should also be broad gauge. Another Select Committee in 1889 warned against extending the metre gauge outside those areas which it already occupied. These areas, where the metre gauge was regarded as the rightful medium of transport, were the regions lying north and NE of the Ganges, the territory south and west of the broad gauge Bombay—Madras line in the South, and Rajputana and Kathiawar in the West.

The recommendations of both these committees were often ignored. By the turn of the century there was a continuous metre-gauge system in the North and West, the networks of Rajputana and Kathiawar being linked with the lines north of the Ganges. However, the substantial metre gauge network of South India was still isolated from the northern group, and so were the lines in Assam. A link between North and South would have been very useful, not only to avoid double transhipment of freight moving from metre-gauge stations in the North to metre-gauge stations in the South, but also to permit pooling of rolling stock. In North India the peak period was April–June, but in the south it was December–April. Largely because of the long-standing fear of creating an all-India metre-gauge system, the link between North and South was not completed until after independence, when the 188-mile Khandwa–Hingoli line was built. Another limitation deliberately imposed on the metre gauge, its exclusion from the big ports, was soon relaxed in the South, but not elsewhere; the metre gauge never gained access to Bombay or Calcutta, but it did penetrate to Madras.

The arguments in favour of the metre gauge could equally well be used to justify gauges smaller than this: If the metre gauge was cheaper than the broad, then the 2ft 6in must be cheaper than metre. The first 2ft 6in gauge railway was a 20-mile feeder line built by the Gaekwar of Baroda to the BBCI main line. It was at first powered by bullocks, but by 1880 was a 40-mile steam railway from which would develop the extensive narrow-gauge system which still serves the Baroda area. In 1880 the first section of the celebrated Darjeeling Himalaya Railway was built, on the 2ft gauge. In ensuing decades a considerable mileage of narrow-gauge lines was laid. Most of these were short, but not all. The Maharajah of Gwalior's 2ft gauge railway developed from a plaything, connecting his palaces and fishing preserves, to a 252-mile system which still serves the area round Gwalior. The Bengal Nagpur Railway built a 625-mile 2ft 6in system in the Nagpur region. The 2ft 6in gauge Barsi Light Railway showed how large the locomotives and rolling stock of a narrow-gauge line could be.

The narrow gauge was not to be spared its own gauge war, the rivals being the 2ft and 2ft 6in standards. This question came to a head in 1897 when the military authorities wanted an assurance that the narrow-gauge strategic railways being built in the NW frontier region would not be without reserves of rolling stock in an emergency. Since such reserves would take the form of stock transferred from other narrow-gauge lines, some uniformity was essential. The local preference was for the 2ft gauge, but the War Department decided to make 2ft 6in the narrow-gauge standard throughout the Empire. Almost all Indian narrow-gauge lines were henceforth built to that gauge.

In terms of capital cost per mile of single track, and including locomotives and rolling stock, construction of broad-gauge lines cost almost exactly double that of metre gauge. In its turn the 2ft 6in gauge could be laid (though probably not to the same standards) at a little more than half the metre-gauge cost, while the 2ft gauge cost a little less than half the metre-gauge cost. As might be expected, operating costs per passenger-mile or ton-mile were lower on the broad gauge, with its higher-capacity vehicles. This advantage, however, was only genuine when traffic was sufficient to fill the broad gauge trains.

The following figures, extracted from J. C. Mackay's *Light Railways for the United Kingdom, India and the Colonies*, may perhaps reflect that author's preference for the narrower gauge, but nonetheless seem to present a picture which is generally accurate for that time. The figures compare the performance of two metre-gauge railways, the Rajputana–Malwa and the Bengal & North Western, with the broad-gauge EIR in 1893.

	EIR	Rajputana Malwa Ry	BNWR
Average passengers per vehicle	18	20	15
Average tons per freight vehicle	6	4	3
Average passengers per train	262	255	248
Average load (tons) per freight train	209	100	97
Engine mile per engine-day	57	48	53
Coal consumption per train mile (lb)	54	31	31

Perhaps the most significant figures in this table are those that reveal that both gauges carried virtually the same number of passengers per train and achieved similar locomotive utilisation rates. Perhaps if different metre-gauge railways had been chosen for comparison the figures might have been more in favour of the broad gauge, but probably not very much more. The broad gauge was at a disadvantage in this kind of comparison because its maximum permitted moving dimensions did not really correspond to its track gauge. Broad-gauge coaches did not exceed 9ft 6in in width, which was 1ft less than European and American vehicles on 4ft 8½in gauge tracks. The metre gauge made much better use of its track width. Although after 1928 wider stock was introduced, the bg loading gauge continued to be restrictive. Standard designs of bg passenger vehicles introduced after 1947 were only 10ft 8in wide, compared with 9ft for new mg stock. Thus the bg ratio of vehicle width to gauge was less than 2:1. On the narrower gauges these ratios were higher: 2.7:1 for mg and about 3:1 in the case of standard stock on 2ft 6in. With freight vehicles the bg had a greater advantage, but this was largely because higher axleloads were permissible, a factor depending not on the gauge but on the choice of engineering standards. Bg speeds also were higher, for similar reasons.

When the mg was first introduced one of the economic arguments revolved around transhipment costs. In the case of passengers, transhipment was not thought a serious problem, for passengers were habituated to changing trains. In the case of freight it was argued that labour costs were so low that transhipment would be very cheap. As the mg developed, break-of-gauge depots were provided with large freight transhipment sheds. These, which are still in use, normally include platforms with bg tracks on one side and mg on the other.

Although the direct cost of transhipment was low, it was soon found that there were other expenses involved, for as is often the case in transport economics, factors which were difficult to define or to determine had been simply left out of the calculation. They included: longer transits, which placed a financial burden on consignors; extra opportunities for pilferage; the need to pack shipments for loading in smaller wagons; and (perhaps most important) reduced wagon utilisation due to the need to keep empties always available at transhipment points. In practice, transhipment stations frequently dealt with as many bg as mg wagons. In 1970–71, for instance, the largest of the 97 break-of-gauge stations (Garhara, near Barauni) dealt with daily averages of 254 bg and 247 mg wagons. This implies a low utilisation of bg capacity.

Even before the first mg lines were laid, it was realised that there would be a gauge problem. But the same judgement can be made of the gauge policy as of the earlier guarantee system. It raised serious problems but it did get railways built which otherwise might have been delayed for years by financial difficulties. The gauge problem itself remained unsolved because of financial stringency. Most experts admitted that at some stage the mg lines would have to be widened. The Robertson Report of 1903 recommended that both bg and mg lines should be re-laid to the 4ft 8½in gauge because such a policy would entail the least difficulties from the loading gauge viewpoint. However, Robertson's opinion did not carry much weight and the assumption remained that the mg would eventually be widened to 5ft 6in. After independence the Indian Government confirmed this policy, and some lines were reconstructed. But it was realised that conversion of the entire mg mileage would be a very long process indeed.

THE RAILWAYS AND THE STATE

As already mentioned, the attempts in the early 1860s to build railways without guarantees had little success. Both the Indian Tramway Company and the Indian Branch Railway Company were soon granted Government guarantees to overcome their financial difficulties. But the Government of India was unwilling to perpetuate the over-generous agreements made with the early railway companies. New agreements were made with the GIP, the BBCI and the Madras railways whereby in exchange for the Government's relinquishment of its right to purchase the companies after 25 years, the companies agreed to pay the Government half of their profits (calculated half-yearly). At the same time the Government decided that in future it would itself finance railway construction. This decision gave great satisfaction to the staff of the Public Works Department (PWD), who were afforded new opportunities for promotion, and was rapidly approved by the British Government, which agreed that £2m might be spent each year on railway building.

From 1869 to 1880 the Government embarked on a number

of key lines, mainly mg, of which the most important were the Rajputana–Malwa, Indus Valley, Northern Bengal, Punjab Northern, and Tirhut Railways. By 1880 the Government had built 2175 miles. Total mileage in that year was nearly 8500. Construction costs of the State lines were considerably lower than those of the private railways built earlier, due not only to the narrower gauge but also to economies in construction. Building was often rapid. For example the 90 mile Rewari-Hissar line was surveyed in March and May 1881, started in October, and opened in June 1883.

During this decade of State construction a private railway lobby developed, especially at Westminster, with the object of restoring Indian railway building to private enterprise. It claimed that State railway managers had less freedom of action. This was hardly true, since they were subordinate to one authority, the Government, whereas private railway managers had to answer to the Government in Calcutta and their boards of directors in London. Economic comparisons were drawn to show that the private railways were more profitable than the State's. These comparisons tended to be unfair, partly because the State railways served less prosperous areas and partly because the EIR was usually chosen to represent the private railways, and the EIR, with its exceptionally dense traffic and cheap local coal, was much more profitable than the average private railway.

Just possibly, if there had been no famines, railway building would have remained a State concern. Famines in India were nothing new. What was new was the Government's determination to do something to avoid and alleviate them. In 1860 a small famine in the NW had been partly alleviated with the help of railways, but in the 1866 Orissa famine the Government, relying on its ideology, held back, confidently expecting the law of supply and demand to bring grain to the stricken area. As a result of one-third of Orissa's population died and the ensuing committee of enquiry recommended extra money for irrigation and railways. Indian famines were not usually the result of a general shortage, but of a shortage (or an

Page 51 (above) An Atlantic of the former GIPR on the Northern Railway near Delhi in 1963; (below) an SPS class 4-4-0 of the former NWR leaves Delhi with a stopping train in 1963

Page 52 (above) Inspection trolley meets an HPS 4–6–0 on the broad gauge near Madras (SR) in 1972; (below) former NWR power and rolling stock on the Pakistan Western Railway at Peshawar in 1963. The 0–6–0 is of Class SGS and the 2–8–0 of class HGS

expected shortage) in a given area; the rich would hoard and the poor would starve because without mechanical transport it was impossible to bring food from surplus areas. The effective range of bullock cart transport was about 50 miles. Beyond that distance the bullocks tended to consume on their trip more grain than they could haul. In any case in famine areas there were few healthy bullocks. During the Madras famine of 1877 grain rotted at stations in the famine areas because there were no bullocks to take it away. In the 1870s the railways were already proving their worth at times of famine. In the 1874 famine, for example, Tirhut was relieved by light railways connecting with Patna, 100 miles away. In the early 1880s a special commission published the Famine Code, which among other things resulted in the building of so-called protective railways.

The need to build famine railways quickly, pressure from Parliament, and the appointment of a new Viceroy (Ripon) who was determined to resurrect private enterprise despite opposition by the Government of India bureaucracy, meant that a new chapter in railway construction began in 1881. In the 1880s three unguaranteed and three guaranteed railway companies were formed. Of the unguaranteed lines the most important was the Bengal & North Western, which survived until 1943 and was the only significant railway to receive no direct Government aid throughout its existence. When it was finally taken over by the State it had 1269 miles of metre gauge track serving the area north of the Ganges and south of Nepal. Of the other two unguaranteed lines one, the Bengal Central, ran into difficulties, was granted a guarantee, and was later absorbed by the Eastern Bengal Railway. The other (the Rohilkhand & Kumaon) received a subsidy for ten years and was taken over by the State at the same time as its neighbour the BNWR. These two railways formed the major part of the present-day North Eastern Railway.

The three new guaranteed companies were the Indian Midland, which connected the GIPR with Agra, Delhi and Jhansi and in 1900 was merged with that railway, and the much larger Bengal Nagpur Railway and Southern Mahratta Railway. The BNR, a broad gauge line, was formed to take over a Government project which had been deferred because of lack of funds; part of its mileage was converted from already-laid metre gauge sections. Its main line ran from an end-to-end junction with the GIPR at Nagpur north east towards Calcutta. It made a junction with the EIR at Asansol, thus providing a shorter route between Bombay and Howrah. In later years it extended in other directions. It built its own line to Howrah. It acquired the northern part of the State-built East Coast Railway (which linked Calcutta with Madras), and extended several branches into the coalfields of Orissa and Bihar.

The Southern Mahratta Railway developed from a famine line into an mg system of more than 1600 miles by the turn of the century. Its north-to-south main line extended from Poona (119 miles from Bombay by GIPR) to Bangalore and Mysore, while its other main line stretched across Southern India from Bezwada on the east coast to Goa on the west, although in Goa its role was that of managing and operating the West of India Portuguese Railway.

In 1892 yet another mg guaranteed railway was begun. This was the Assam Bengal, most of which was to be acquired by Pakistan in 1947. Like the immediately preceding guaranteed companies, the terms of its contract were considerably less burdensome to the Government than those of the first guaranteed railways. At this period the guaranteed interest offered to the companies had fallen to 3 or 3½ per cent, and the companies were required to pay to the Government (or, strictly speaking, the Secretary of State for India) up to three-quarters of their profits. Meanwhile, the Government was gradually buying up the older private companies in accordance with its contractual rights as expressed in the various agreements. Payment was either by the handing over of specially issued Indian Government stock, or by Government annuities. In most cases the old companies were reconstituted and continued to manage and operate their former lines in accordance with new contracts. The fate of the main railways is summarised in the next paragraph.

In the NE, the Sind, Punjab & Delhi was placed under direct Government management after purchase; because it served strategic areas, the Government insisted that it should not be worked by a private operating company. Together with the Indus Valley line and other railways in the Punjab and NW areas it was reconstituted as the State-operated North Western Railway, connecting Delhi with Amritsar, Lahore, Karachi and (later) the Khyber Pass.The Eastern Bengal and the Oudh & Rohilkhand were likewise taken under direct State management. However, most of the large private railways were placed, after State purchase, under the management of private working companies. These companies, which in effect were the old companies, were granted contracts which, compared to the old guarantee agreements, entailed a reduction of the capital held by the companies in the respective railways. (this was because the companies had relinquished the fixed assets, retaining only the operating plant and equipment) a reduction of the rate of interest guaranteed by the Government on the companies' remaining capital, and increased shares for the Government in the companies' profits. The railways which sooner or later came into this category were the EIR (the first to be taken over, in 1879), the GIP, BBCI. South Indian, Southern Mahratta and Bengal Nagpur. Of the lines which remained in private ownership, only the BNW and the Rohilkhand & Kumaon were significant. The Madras Railway, one of the early big companies, was taken over by the State in 1907 and attached to the Southern Mahratta to form the Madras & Southern Mahratta Railway.

The foregoing refers to only the most important railways, and only briefly. The history of railway construction, ownership and management in India would need a multi-volume survey. Railways were continually being formed, built, amalgamated, bought up, and sold and amalgmation and reorganisation are likely to continue. By 1921 there were no fewer than 175 railway undertakings in India. The Government sometimes transferred sections of one railway to another if it considered this advisable for political or economic reasons. For example, in 1925 the State-operated Oudh & Rohilkhand Railway was amalgamated with the EIR, while the latter's Jabalpur branch was transferred to the GIPR and its line from Ghaziabad eastwards to Delhi and Kalka transferred to the NWR.

The Government of India was not the only public authority to build railways. The railways of the Gaekwar of Baroda, already mentioned, were far from being the only examples of railways built by the Indian princes for the benefit of their territories. In 1870 the Nizam of Hyderabad paid for a railway linking Hyderabad with the GIPR. It was to be worked, managed and built by the British Government under the supervision of the British Resident in Hyderabad. Similarly, the Maharajah of Indore financed a railway to connect Indore with the GIPR. By 1950, when they were absorbed by Indian Railways, the Princely States' railways totalled about 7000 miles, of which about 1000 miles were worked by the adjacent main-line railways. The largest among them was the Nizam of Hyderabad's State Railway, which had grown to 1375 miles.

Although the Indian government had some powers to supervise safety matters, in general these railways were genuinely independent. At the other end of the scale, local district boards or small companies built a multitude of short lines from their own resources. To encourage the laying of such lines, the Government offered to companies special terms ('branch-line terms'). The first version of these terms offered the branch-line companies up to 10 per cent of the earnings gained by the main line companies from traffic which had originated or terminated on the branch line. This rebate would be fixed annually so that, together with the branch line's direct earnings, a 4 per cent dividend could be paid on capital. There were several modifications between the initial terms of 1893 and the final terms of 1914. In essence, later changes enabled the branch companies to choose between a small unconditional guarantee of interest on capital, or a rebate on interchanged traffic which would be expected to permit a dividend at a rather higher rate (typically a 3½ per cent guarantee or a 5 per cent dividend made up of the branch's profits plus the rebate). Additional light railways were built by local district boards, financed either by taxation or by offers of their own guarantees of interest to private companies.

Somewhat alarmed by the multiplicity of lines and terms which it had brought into being since 1849, and doubting whether similar methods could continue in the future, the Government of India in 1901 asked the British Government to send out a railway expert to advise on the situation. This was by no means the last time overseas advice was requested; in future years there were to be, among others, the Mackay Committee (1908), the Acworth Committee (1921), and the Wedgwood Committee (1937). In general, the reports of these committees said nothing startling, but their prestige gave their recommendations great weight, so that measures for which local men had been vainly pleading suddenly became acceptable.

The case of the Robertson Report of 1903 is somewhat different. Robertson appears to be one of those experts who became so familiar in the mid-twentieth century: men of no particular talent but regarded with some awe in underdeveloped countries because they had been sent out by the Government of a country reputed to be advanced. Robertson, however, had a harder time than his successors. Unlike them, he had to deal with a Viceroy (Curzon) who had the intelligence to see through him, the industry to test his conclusions, and the self-confidence to criticise him. When after months of agreeable all-expenses-paid travel Robertson presented his report, an ill-written string of platitudes, Curzon immediately cancelled his free passage home and requested him to produce something better. Eventually, with the help of an official nominated by Curzon, the Robertson Report was made fit for printing. It rather resembles the work of a first-year undergraduate, but it does provide a useful summary of the situation of Indian railways in 1902.

In that year, reported Robertson, there were 25,936 miles open, worked by 33 railway administrations; twenty-three of these administrations were companies, controlling 17,754 miles; five were princely States with 2,184 miles; and five were Government, with 5,998 miles. (At this time the process of buying out the private companies was not quite finished). Most of the mileage (20,474) was the financial responsibility of the Government; it owned and worked 8,638 miles, it owned but leased to working companies another 4,615 miles, and it guaranteed the interest on 7,321 miles of companies' lines. Of the remaining 5,462 miles, for which the Government had no financial responsibility, 1,104 miles had been financed by companies without Government assistance apart from free land, 350 miles were financed by companies with subsidies or guarantees from local bodies, 766 miles had been built by companies under the 'rebate' terms, and 3,242 were owned or financed by the Princely States. Apart from the BBCIR, whose contract was terminable in 1905, and the Madras Railway (terminable 1907), there were two other lines whose contracts seemed over-generous. The Southern Mahratta's quarter-share of profits was calculated on net earnings *before* deduction of capital charges, so that railway had little incentive to econo- mise on capital expenditure. The Assam Bengal Railway, whose contract was not terminable until 1921, had such a large capital expenditure and such low receipts that a profit seemed out of the question. It therefore had no incentive either to reduce expenditure or increase income, being content to rely on the Government guarantee to provide a three per cent return.

Government supervision of those lines for which it had no financial responsibility was in practice confined to an annual inspection and to investigations of accidents. State-managed railways were headed by managers who had fairly wide powers, not being subordinated to consulting engineers. How- ever, State railway officials, being Government employees, were subject to frequent transfer, and this sometimes led to poor management. The Eastern Bengal Railway, for example, had seven changes of manager between 1898 and 1902. A grievance of State railway officials was that their salaries were lower than those of their counterparts on company lines. The latter, however, were subject to much greater supervision. Managers of companies working State lines were responsible not only to their boards of directors in London, but also to the British Government (through the Secretary of State in Council, the Government Director nominated to the board, and the consulting engineer), and to the Government of India (through the Governor General in Council, the Railway Branch of the PWD, and one of the seven Government consulting engineers). Of these, the consulting engineers seem to have raised the most hackles; they were accused of unnecessary interference and of being inaccessible in their summer hill stations. Another cause for complaint was that money for capital expenditure on most lines for which the Government had financial responsibility came from an annual 'programme', whose scope was determined by current economic conditions. Not only did this mean that the amount made available could not be foreseen; it meant also that a proportion of it would never be spent, for unspent allocations lapsed at the end of each financial year. Under these conditions efficient and long term planning was impossible.

Even before World War I there were signs of under-capacity and this problem was accentuated by the war. After 1918 railway deficiencies seemed indefensible, and there was a growing demand for nationalisation. The coal trade, and hence the iron and steel industry, was hampered by inadequate rail service. In 1918 the textile city of Nagpur was receiving cotton up to six months late. In 1921 jute mills had to close because of the non-arrival of coal supplies. Export orders were being lost. Grain was reported to be rotting at the railway stations. The result of public disquiet was the arrival in India in 1921 of the Acworth Committee, which was to enquire into the management, finance, control and organisation of the railways.

The situation which the Committee found was as follows

(March 1921 figures): the Government of India, together with small mileages attributable to provincial or local governments, owned 26,889 route miles, but worked only 8,929; the Princely States owned 4,394 miles and worked 2,889; while private companies owned only 5,746 miles but worked 25,211. Of the companies which worked Government-owned lines, all had their headquarters in London, whereas of the companies working privately-owned railways, most were domiciled in India.

Thus by far the greater part of the mileage was operated by London-based companies whose boards were represented in India by the managers (known as 'agents') of the respective undertakings. Each company's directors included one nominee of the British Government, but most were former servants of the Indian Government, who had retired to Britain on pension. They had the advantage of local experience, but their method of appointment was unsatisfactory. They were co-opted by the boards and served until they chose to withdraw, a circumstance which meant that seniority and senility went hand in hand. These old men, however, enjoyed great influence. Being domiciled near the Secretary of State for India, they could often gain his support on matters in which they were opposed by the Government of India.

Several Viceroys had complained about this, but with little result. In 1867, for example, the British Government compelled the Government of India to allow the Madras Railway to increase its fares, although this was against Indian Government policy. Again, in 1892 the Secretary of State agreed to the contract with the Assam Bengal Railway, whose terms the Indian Government disapproved. In India day-to-day control of the railways had formerly been exercised by the PWD Railway Branch, but after the Robertson and Mackay Reports this was changed. A three-man Railway Board was established which with its supporting staff formed the Railway Department. This was under the Railway Member of the Legislative Council, but the President of the Railway Board had direct access to the Viceroy. Consulting engineers were replaced by railway inspectors. Although this new system was an improvement it was not everywhere popular. The Railway Board tended to be loaded with detail and its members, who were experienced railwaymen, did not respond very sympathetically to public grievances; the deplorable conditions of third-class travel could be largely ascribed to this indifference.

The main results of the Acworth Committee were the decisions to take over the working of those railways still operated by companies, to separate railway finance from general finance, and to improve the system of Government control. The Committee's recommendation on the State's takeover was debated in the Legislative Assembly in 1923, where the 'unofficial' Members (increasingly important and largely representing non-European opinion) were solidly in favour of the proposal.

The first working companies to be taken over, on the termination of their contracts, were the GIP and EIR in 1925. The remaining big companies were taken over in 1942, 1943 and 1944, leaving only some of the Princely State railways and various short lines to be worked by non-Governmental undertakings. Financially, the main result of the Acworth Report was that from 1924 the railway budget was presented separately from the general budget in the Legislative Assembly, and railway finance was separate from general finance, although a contribution by the railways to the general finances had a prior claim on the railways' net revenue; this contribution could be regarded as interest paid on capital. Henceforth the railway budget was less subject to economy drives imposed by the Financial Member of the Legislative Assembly; after making its percentage contribution to general revenue the Railway Board was free to allocate its revenue as it wished. As for control, the Railway Board was enlarged after the Acworth Report, but subsequent modifications suggest that it still proved unsatisfactory. From 1937 there was a Minister for Transport & Communications. The Minister could intervene in any matter dealt with by the Railway Board, but in practice most matters were decided by the latter. The Minister was a civil servant and remained so after independence; only in the early 1950s did this office become the preserve of successful politicians.

FREIGHT SERVICES

About two thirds of the Indian railways' revenue came from freight traffic, although individual railways might vary quite widely from this average. The pattern of traffic changed slowly over the decades, parallel with changes in the Indian economy, but it is fair to say that foodgrains and coal were the two largest items of freight throughout the period from 1870 to 1947 and after, Foodgrain traffic, which tended to fluctuate from year to year, was on average the biggest item of freight by weight, and very much the biggest by revenue. Then came coal and coke which, because so much of it moved fairly short distances, from the coalfields of Bengal and Orissa to Calcutta, produced less revenue than the tonnage figures suggested. After these two categories came various bulk raw materials such as oilseed, salt, jute, and sugar.

As was the case elsewhere in the world before road competition developed, freight transits were slow. At the turn of the century, for example, freight trains between Howrah and Lucknow averaged about 4 mph (although the Howrah-Delhi trains were more than twice as fast as this). These speeds were improved only marginally in succeeding decades. However, as with passenger services, the customer was less concerned with train speeds than with other factors such as reliability, convenience, and costs. In these respects the railways' freight services earned much criticism. In fact it was probably business interests, rightly or wrongly feeling that they were not getting a fair deal, which were the loudest and most effective critics of the railways. Partly perhaps because of the absence of competition, but largely because shortage of capacity in relation to demand enabled railway managers to adopt a take-it-or-leave-it attitude, freight consignors did not receive the best possible service.

The service offered to the coal industry by the EIR was notorious at times. This railway had given the development of the coal industry pride of place in its initial prospectuses, but once built, and with the mineowners quite dependent on it, it exploited its monopoly position as far as it could; presumably only the fear of Government intervention limited its indifference to complaint. Coal shipments to Calcutta were subjected to high tariffs, and a fair proportion of every shipment disappeared in transit. How much this loss was due to organised pilferage, and how much to overloaded rolling stock, remained unclear; what rankled was the EIR's refusal to weigh wagons at the end of the journey as well as at the beginning. The coal industry was not only losing coal, but was compelled to pay for movement transport of consignments that never arrived at destination. Towards the end of the century the EIR belatedly discovered that lower tariffs could bring forth disproportionately more traffic, and rates were moderated. But coal merchants were still expected to behave themselves; wagons arriving in the morning had to be unloaded and released by evening if stiff demurrage penalties were to be avoided.

This coal traffic also illustrates the crucial influence on Indian economic development of railway freight tariffs. Because of high rates, the Eastern coal industry found it cheaper to send coal to Bombay by sea via Calcutta rather than by rail throughout. Thus instead of a direct 1150-mile southwesterly route with no transhipment, the coal was first sent 180 miles eastwards to Calcutta docks (with a troublesome crossing of the Hooghly), then 2,080 miles by a roundabout sea route. It is easy to see how much the market for Indian coal was restricted by high rail tariffs, and why it was better for several consumers to import British coal than to use the indigenous product.

However, a pinch of salt should be kept handy when reading certain post-independence studies of railway tariffs in the Imperial era, for too many of their authors seem to believe that political commitment is an adequate compensation for academic mediocrity. When it becomes possible to study this question impartially, it will probably be found that while railway tariff policies did hold back certain developments, they stimulated others. For example, while it is true that the ports had very favourable railway tariffs, so that exports of raw materials to Britain and imports of manufactures from Britain were favoured, it might be argued that these low rates favoured economic activity in the inland centres, for which distance from a port became a less expensive handicap. Moreover, in the period between the world wars special rates were introduced specifically to help Indian industry combat competition from imports; iron and steel, and cement, were among the industries which benefitted from these. In general, during the British period there was an underlying conflict between the Government and the railways on tariff matters. The Government prefered low freight and passenger tariffs, regarding the railways as a means to economic development, while the railways preferred the opposite, having profit as the prime, though not sole, consideration. From 1862, starting in Bombay, the Government began to fix maximum rates. Later it intervened in so-called staple traffic rates (grain, coal, third and fourth class passengers). On the other hand, in 1869 the Secretary of State, no doubt influenced by the London directors of the various companies, sponsored rate increases against the advice of the Viceroy.

Despite Government planning of the railway routes, competition did appear, especially after the longer mg lines were built. In the south the SMR between Poona and Bangalore offered a short cut, albeit with break-of-gauge, for Bombay-Madras traffic hitherto moving over the GIP/Madras Railway bg route. When the Rajputana-Malwa Railway completed the mg Delhi/Agra–Ahmedabad route, connecting with the BBCI Ahmedabad–Bombay bg line, traffic which hitherto had moved over the EIR to Calcutta was attracted to Bombay. Agra for example was almost equidistant from the two ports, and Bombay's port charges and freight rates to Europe were cheaper.

When the GIPR, through its associated Indian Midland Railway, gained access to Cawnpore, even more of the EIR hinterland was threatened. But the EIR's costs per ton-mile were only about half those of its rivals. Fierce rate-cutting developed, the EIR accusing its rivals of charging less than their costs. In 1887 the Government intervened, setting maximum and minimum rates for Indian freight traffic. The EIR complained that the minima were too high, because its costs were so low that it could charge less than the minima and still make a profit, even though other railways could not. Thus, it claimed, the traffic was not being shared between Calcutta and Bombay in the most efficient way. The EIR also faced competition from Ganges river craft; fortunately, its off-peak season coincided with the most favourable season for river shipping and it was able to embarrass most river operators by offering low seasonal 'monsoon rates.'

In the inter-war period especially the tariff question received much attention, perhaps because a critical and well-informed Indian public opinion was being increasingly felt. In 1924 a Rates Tribunal was established to revise charges, and almost simultaneously, to meet public complaints, a Rates Advisory Committee was set up to protect the public from the more obvious abuses of the system. All freight was distributed between six classifications, and for each classification the Railway Board fixed the maximum and the minimum rate; between these upper and lower limits the railways fixed the rates at their discretion, on the 'what the traffic will bear' principle.

At the turn of the century the standard freight wagon tare was about six tons with a capacity of 12 tons. On the EIR, however, mineral traffic was being carried in vacuum-braked four-wheelers of eight tons tare, sixteen tons capacity. The same railway was operating 1000-ton freight trains, although elsewhere in India 700 tons was a more typical maximum on flat sections. The GIPR ran 700-ton trains on the flat, 470-ton trains on hilly sections, and limited trains crossing the Ghats to 370 tons.

As time passed, bigger locomotives permitted heavier loads; by the 1920s the BNR was running 2000-ton coal trains hauled by Garratt locomotives.

PASSENGER SERVICES

As the decades passed, public criticism of the Indian railways both intensified and received more attention from the authorities. But there were relatively few complaints about the speeds of passenger trains. Critics were more concerned about the amenities of travel, about corruption, and about freight tariffs and schedules. Yet by European standards at least, passenger train speeds remained low. From the operating point of view this was advantageous, for the introduction of high-speed trains on heavily-trafficked main lines, largely single-track, would have necessitated many operating complexities including passing of slower trains in refuge sidings, with consequent delays.

It was not on the main lines that the most snail-like trains ran, but on the secondary lines and branches. Lethargic schedules did not irritate the third-class traveller, who was more concerned with obtaining a seat, while Europeans and wealthier or more influential Indians travelled in the superior classes whose comforts did much to compensate for long transits. It has to be remembered, too, that government planning of the railway network had meant that there were few pairs of population centres served by competing routes. The only 'railway race' witnessed in India was sporadic rivalry between the BBCI and GIP, both of which operated a bg Bombay–Delhi service. The existence of two routes between Bombay and Calcutta caused little competitive schedule-pairing, possibly because the GIP handled the western sectors of both routes; in 1914 the shorter route via Nagpur and the BNR offered the passenger a journey which was actually 5½ hr longer (though cheaper) than that offered by the original EIR route via Allahabad, although by the 1920s the BNR route was marginally faster.

Traditionally, the trains connecting with the P&O sailings at Bombay were regarded as the crack services of the Indian railways. The Suez Canal had been opened in 1869. and by Edwardian times mail services had brought Bombay to within 13 days of London. Every Friday evening at the turn of the century a traveller could leave Cannon Street Station in London and proceed via Calais to Brindisi. From here a small P&O steamer would take him to Port Said, where he would transfer to a larger P&O liner for the rest of the trip. On board this ship the Indian mail would be sorted, ready for distribution on arrival at Bombay. From the GIP Victoria Terminus in Bombay every Friday a special connecting train, carrying first class passengers and mail only, would take the traveller onwards to Calcutta (Howrah) at an average speed of about 35 mph.

In the early 1920s the GIP was operating boat trains from Bombay to Madras and Delhi in addition to Calcutta, and thanks to some competition from the BBCI, the once-weekly GIP Delhi service was the country's fastest train, taking only 27hr 10min for the southbound run of 957 miles; with 18 intermediate stops, and the speed restrictions of the Ghat section to be negotiated, this timing was justifiably regarded by the GIP as cause for pride. The corresponding service to Calcutta (1350 miles) took 36½ hrs, a considerable improvement over the 64hr allowed 50 years earlier for the 1400 miles run.

Another fast service operated by the GIP was a summer train between Bombay and Poona, largely for the benefit of horseracing enthusiasts. In 1901 this covered the 119 miles in 3hr 26min, including two engine changes and a reversal on the Ghat section. Elsewhere in India the better bg services were scheduled at around 30mph. On the Oudh & Rohilkhand for example, in 1911 the Punjab Mail (Peshawar–Moghal Sarai) ran 519 miles in 18hr 20min, including 2hr 40min spent at intermediate halts. At the same period the 547-mile BNR section of the Madras–Calcutta route was covered by the fastest train in 20hr 15min.

Mg speeds were considerably lower. Possibly the smartest service was that of the South Indian Railway from Madras to Tuticorin, connecting with the boat to Ceylon. As early as 1898 this train was formed of vestibuled coaches in both first and second class, and took 21hr 50min for the 443 miles.

Fifteen years later it was moving at the same speed. Perhaps more typical of the mg was the MSM's Poona–Bangalore service, which in the early years of the century was allowed 36hr 25min for the 625 miles. This train boasted not only bogie coaches but also gas lighting, although in common with that railway's other trains it lacked automatic brakes.

The so-called race to Delhi was run in 1927, when the BBCI P&O Punjab Special competed with the GIP's Bombay–Delhi boat mail. The BBCI Bombay–Delhi bg route dated from 1909. when its Baroda–Muttra link was completed. From Muttra to the outskirts of Delhi it had running powers over the GIP main line. The BBCI route was about 90 miles shorter than that of the GIP and not hampered by any Ghat sections. Thus the BBCI could cut the Bombay–Delhi schedule of this once-weekly train to less than 24hr. The following year, the excitement having palled, the BBCI again attracted attention by introducing its daily Frontier Mail, which between Bombay and Delhi ran according to the schedule of the previous year's boat mail: 23hr 35min for 865 miles.

In the mid-1930s the GIP could still claim to operate India's fastest train. This was the Deccan Queen, which covered the 119 miles up the Ghats to Poona in 2¾hr, reeling off the first 62 miles at an average speed of 52mph.

The BBCI however, still led on the Bombay–Delhi route. The Frontier Mail ran what was by then 861 miles in 23hr 50min, an overall average of 36mph. The GIP's competing Punjab Mail ran the 956 miles to Delhi in 29hr 38min with 30 stops. Elsewhere in India another Punjab Mail, that of the EIR and NWR from Calcutta to Lahore, averaged 33mph. Schedules in the last year of British rule were still suffering from wartime difficulties, but in 1946 the Deccan Queen was still India's fastest train even though by then it took 3hrs, and its initial 52mph dash had deteriorated to 48mph. The best BBCI and GIP trains from Bombay to Delhi averaged 33mph and 31mph, respectively. The Bombay–Calcutta mails averaged 29mph via the BNR and 32mph by the longer route. The Calcutta–Madras mail averaged 25mph, while the best mg train from Ahmedabad to Delhi on the BBCI was scheduled at 23mph.

Page 69 (above) Canadian-built CWD 2–8–2 on a CR freight at Agra in 1963; (below) A WM 2–6–4T takes the heavily loaded Monghyr branch train out of Jamalpur (ER) in 1972

Page 70 (above) One of the ill-fated XB Pacifics, relegated to Madras suburban service, at work in 1972; (below) a WP Pacific is steamed after overhaul at the CR Parel (Bombay) Works in 1972. An XA light Pacific is in steam on the right

Schedules of many trains tended to remain unchanged for years, but punctuality was reasonably good (the best year was probably 1935–6, with 87 per cent of all trains arriving on time). Since company managers needed the approval of their directors before making train service innovations, small improvements in schedules were probably not considered worth the trouble of the correspondence they would entail.

Really high-speed services seemed out of the question, with the apparently unavoidable frequent and lengthy halts en route. These intermediate stops were not merely for exchanging passengers; they were used to water the engines and clean their fires, and to provide meal breaks. It was considered impracticable to provide on the trains dining facilities which would satisfy all caste and other religious scruples. Thus it was customary to halt the trains for about half-an-hour at the midday and evening meal times, and for about a quarter-of-an-hour for breakfast. In addition there were speed restrictions which precluded long stops being compensated by high-speed running; 60mph was the bg and 45mph the mg limit and there were of course sections on which the limits were considerably lower.

On the branch lines trains were slow, often averaging considerably less than 10mph and (especially if they were mixed trains) liable to take many hours longer than the timetable allowed.

Suburban services developed quite rapidly in the large cities. In 1901 the GIP was operating 36 pairs of Bombay inner-suburban trains, but ten years later its Bombay–Kalyan line was served by about 60 trains, of which all but a handful were commuter services. The latter, typically six-coach trains hauled by 0–6–2 tank engines, covered the 34 miles in 64min, with 19 intermediate halts. In the 1920s, after electrification, this service became faster and more frequent.

AMENITIES

At the turn of the century the average Indian passenger train carried 1.31 first class passengers, 4.86 second, 10.65 intermediate ('inter') class and 186.6 third class. These numbers, and especially the preponderance of third class passengers, did not change radically over the next half-century. There were, of course, differences between railways; many railways did not provide 'inter' class accommodation and some, like the GIP and EIR, had large commuter operations which affected their averages. GIP trains carried an average of 2.08 first class passengers, whereas the SIR (the largest passenger carrier) only averaged .85.

First class travellers were provided with spacious compartments which contained one, two or three lower, and one, two or three foldaway upper berths. The lavatory which adjoined each compartment included a shower and, on some railways, a small bath. Electric fans were beginning to appear. One traditional cooling apparatus consisted of wet mats overhanging the windows, moistened by roof tanks. In the hot season the wise traveller also provided himself with large quantities of ice; death from heatstroke was always a possibility. In 1915 32 British soldiers died in a NWR troop train which ventured forth without ice or fans in a shade temperature of 125 deg F.

During meal breaks the first class passenger received in his compartment a tray from the station dining room carrying the European or Indian food which he had ordered, via the guard by telegram some hours previously.

When restaurant cars were introduced the traveller could have his meals sent down to his compartment in the same way, or he could walk up to the restaurant car and eat in comfort, returning to his compartment at a suitable halt. Vestibuled stock was for many years rare, as were corridors. Many travellers took their own servants with them on a journey, and it was these who looked after them. When passengers had to change trains, the first-class waiting rooms provided a theoretically clean and cool refuge. For passengers requiring privacy, most railways offered special rates for exclusive occupancy of a compartment. The two-berth *coupé* compartment was also coming into favour, especially with married couples.

Some railways introduced fourth-class accommodation after 1874. This was without seats, but in 1885 in response to criticism seats were provided. At the same time, however, the fourth class was renamed third, and the third reclassified as inter; so a four-class system survived on many lines. First-class fares were about double second class, and four to six times higher than third. Third class fares were very low indeed. Despite high first class fares it is doubtful whether first-class passenger travel was ever remunerative for the railways. The third-class passenger provided the profits. On average, between 1925 and 1939 nine-tenths of passenger revenue came from third-class ticket sales, and third-class fares covered costs by about eight times. Minimal costs per passenger mile were obtained by packing third-class passengers tight and offering them few facilities. In the inter-War years, when all classes of travel declined, most railways (and especially company-operated railways) continued to improve first-class accommodation in preference to offering more third-class seat-miles, even though third-class travel was grievously overcrowded. There was a lamentable tendency on the part of railwaymen to despise the third-class passengers who were indeed sometimes dirty, dishonest and unco-operative. The majority were not, and many of those who seemed to be unpleasant were really only bewildered or fearful or ignorant. In retrospect, it is hard to justify the distinction implied in the 'Reserved for Ladies' notices attached to certain first and second class compartments and the 'Women Only' labels on third class accommodation. Nor was it helpful when railwaymen referred to first class waiting *rooms* and third class waiting *sheds*, even though the quality of the facilities provided did perhaps give ground for this semantic distinction.

As Indian representation in political life was extended, public complaints about third class travel received more attention. One of the first Indian nationalist organisations, as early as the 1870s agitated with some success for the provision of lavatories in third-class coaches. However, this was a slow process, by 1941 only the NWR had latrines in all its third class coaches. The BNWR, which had very low fares, very slow trains, and very poorly-paid staff, still had 42 per cent of its coaches unequipped by 1939. The NWR was State-owned and worked, whereas the BNWR was privately owned and operated; in general the State railways provided better facilities than the private lines, probably because they were more sensitive to criticism expressed in the Legislature. Passengers in trains lacking toilet facilities had to do the best they could at the trackside or at the latrines provided at stations. Station latrines often deterred passengers, and were condemned by Gandhi as defying description, '. . . The army of flies buzzing about them warns you against their use . . . I know passengers who fast while they are travelling just in order to lessen the misery . . .' Gandhi made a point of travelling third class. He had some comments on a trip he made in 1917 on the Bombay–Madras mail, in a 22-seat compartment:

> The guards or other railway servants came in only to push in more passengers. A defiant Menon merchant protested against this packing of passengers like sardines. In vain did he say that this was his fifth night on the train. The guard insulted him and referred him to the management at the terminus. There were during this time as many as 35 passengers in the carriage during the greater part of it. Some lay on the floor in the midst of dirt, and some had to keep standing. A free fight was at one time avoided only by the intervention of some of the older passengers . . .

It had been the practice to run only first and second class coaches through in long distance trains. Third-class passengers were usually compelled to take slow trains, or a succession of trains, although this situation improved after the turn of the century. It was not unusual for third-class passengers, especially the ignorant or illiterate, to be compelled to pay bribes to railway staff and railway policemen. Sometimes the lower railway staff, anxious to assert their superiority over at least somebody, or genuinely finding a passenger troublesome, would resort to violence.

Another cause for complaint was the railways' alleged failure to provide food and water for third-class passengers. Here there were real problems. With two major religions, several influential sects, each with its own rules as to purity of water and food, besides the Hindu caste system, it was not easy to satisfy everyone. The railways did provide water carriers at the main stations, who would perambulate the platforms dispensing water from skin bottles, but even this facility had its problems. High-caste Hindus demanded the certainty that nobody of certain inferior castes had touched their water, and before refilling their brass pots might inquire lengthily into the pedigree of the carrier.

With food there were additional difficulties, although the provision of private vegetarian foodstalls did at one stroke provide sustenance not only for the many vegetarians but also for those who would not eat beef and for those who would not eat pork.

Restaurant cars, for reasons already mentioned, were slow to appear. In 1901 the Oudh & Rohilkhand Railway was the only bg line to operate restaurant cars, and this only in its mail train. On the mg, the best train of the Rajputana–Malwa included a diner for part of its run; and the Assam Bengal Railway's Chittagong–Silchar Mail was also served by a diner. The Southern Mahratta Railway's Poona–Bangalore mg train was soon added to this short list. In later decades refreshment cars became more common and towards the end of British rule there were Hindu and/or Muslim refreshment cars in many trains, including the fastest.

THE RAILWAY THIEF

Passenger coaches built for Indian railways incorporated decades of experience in dealing with railway thieves. Over the years many ideas were tried, some successful and some not. An example of the latter was the device which at night automatically illuminated the sides of passengers trains as soon as they fell below a certain speed; this was tried by the Eastern Bengal Railway in an effort to prevent the access and escape of train thieves. Among the more successful practices, embodied in modern rolling stock were barred windows, shutters and doors which were lockable from the inside of compartments, and the absence of continuous external running boards on non-corridor stock. Thanks to these practices, and an effort to improve police work, railway thieves are less of a menace now than they were in the early part of the century. They exist still, but lack the zest, skill and cunning of their predecessors.

Railway thieves could be classified into three groups: pickpockets, dishonest railwaymen, and the tribes of professional thieves. Pickpockets usually worked alone. They tended to include individuals of all castes, although many dressed themselves in upper caste style to disarm suspicion. Those who frequented stations sometimes masqueraded as pedlars (and genuine station pedlars often acted as their receivers). A favourite hunting ground was (and is) the crowds milling around ticket office windows. Others worked the trains, either by travelling as ordinary passengers or by walking along the outside footboards while the train was in motion, inserting their hands to remove or rifle bags and jackets hanging on pegs. Some of these operators did not hesitate to use violence against passengers found alone in compartments, and a number of victims had their throats cut or were thrown out of the train. Towards 1914 this kind of criminal, in quest of higher productivity, was tending to form gangs of train robbers. The SIR, which had perhaps unwisely introduced corridor trains, was especially troubled in 1914 by one such gang, apparently led by women. A few years earlier a similar gang had been uncovered at Poona which for no less than twenty years had been robbing GIPR and MSMR trains.

Much of the thieving done by railwaymen belongs to the category of corruption, and will be described in a later chapter. Railwaymen were in an excellent situation, and were much sought after by outside criminals for the information which they could pass. Sometimes they would go further. Marshalling yard staff, for example, might move a wagon containing a valuable consignment to a remote siding, where it could be burgled at leisure. Signalmen might halt trains for the same purpose at night on remote stretches of line. Thieving train guards, because they changed runs so frequently, were especially hard to detect. At Bangalore at least in 1896 and 1897 the so-called 'Golden Gang' of train guards was spectacularly successful in removing silks and lace from boxes sent by train. Wine imports moving from Bombay were also at risk; as soon as any consignment was 'discovered' to have been tampered with, any guard to whom it was subsequently entrusted could take a swig with a clear conscience. Stationmasters, having greater responsibilities, had correspondingly greater opportunities. One such official at a small station on the East Coast line, anxious to win the 'best-kept station' competition, ordered rare plants from a distant horticultural institute, using a fictitious name. When they arrived at his station he planted them and informed the sender that the addressee could not be traced. As he expected, the horticultural institute then asked him to dispose of them by auction on its behalf. This he did, auctioning them to himself at a bargain price. By the 1930s the situation was probably no worse than previously, and it was certainly better than it would become in the war years. By the 1930s too, the depredations of the professional railway robber gangs were well under control, and they never seemed likely to regain the importance they had in the early part of the century. These gangs, or rather tribes, had their origins in the pre-railway age and their traditions were those of the *Thugs*. The *Thugs*, who had combined propitiation of the goddess Kali, by means of ritual murder, with the material benefits of highway robbery, had a hard time in the nineteenth century, for British policy had been directed towards their extermination, with some success, so that unapprehended thugs turned to the new railways as less perilous fields of endeavour. Other outlaw tribes followed their example, and in ensuing decades large-scale organised railway robbery was mainly in the hands of seven different tribes, each of which devoted its entire life and culture to the task.

Each of these tribes had its speciality, but there were also features in common (including, eventually, registration under the 1911 Criminal Tribes Act). They all had a permanent base in their tribal village, which was usually well equipped with hiding places for stolen goods and fugitives from justice. At all times a proportion of the active population would be away, working a selected part of the railway network; another proportion would be serving sentences in gaol. Capital required for mounting operations came typically from rich old men of the tribe, retired from active service. Most operatives were highly trained, having been apprenticed to the trade at an early age. All made good use of their womenfolk; using them in particular as hiding places for stolen jewels. They had various techniques of secret communication, sometimes by signs and sometimes by their own impenetrable slang.

Among the tools of their trade was paint, with which they could decorate themselves with misleading caste marks. They also carried that essential of the self-respecting Indian thief, a small pair of scissors with which to cut out money and jewels tied in their victims' clothing. They were trained to carry small scissors and knives in their mouths. The most professional of these thieves, living in the Deccan, despatched gangs of about a dozen operatives to selected areas of the railway network. These gangs would rent a house in the chosen locality as their base, and then work the trains in small groups, posing as pilgrims.

Their *modus operandi* was to enter compartments in pairs. At night one of the pair would lie on the floor while his seated companion, wrapping himself loosely in a large blanket, would contrive to cover the activities proceeding at floor level. The latter consisted of the opening, by means of a sharp knife hidden between gum and upper lip, of any bags placed by passengers under the seat. The booty would be handed to the seated friend and both would then leave the train, but not before sewing up the rifled baggage. Another tribe, directly descended from the Thugs, were the Koravars, who specialised in station platform activity. They were originally of inferior caste, and reputed to eat all kinds of unpleasant food, such as crows and squirrels. The railways however brought them such chances of enrichment that they began to dress and act like members of the superior castes. Very superstitious, they would abandon their operations if their path was crossed by a cat or a widow. Rather appropriately, they worshipped not Kali but the Goddess of Sleep, praying that she would imbue their intended victims with slumber. They specialised in bag-stealing. They carried their own bags, stuffed with rags, which they would place alongside a traveller's bag and at a suitable moment they would move off, leaving their own bag but picking up the other. They kidnapped children at about five years of age, and gave them a three-year course in their traditional techniques of theft. Their womenfolk were pro-miscuous, but never became involved with men of superior castes as they feared that any resulting children might inherit traces of honesty.

Perhaps the most accomplished thieves came from a tribe near Aligarh. In the cool season these men cultivated rose plantations, and were skilled in the use of a particularly long-nosed secateur. In summer they took these secateurs with them on railway expeditions, and would imperceptibly snip off the necklaces and bangles of sleeping passengers. The more experienced, faced with victims asleep in an inconvenient position, would tickle the soles of their feet with a feather until they turned.

The disappearance of these gangs was probably a conse-quence of more active police intervention. In their heyday, robbers habitually carried a few rupees to bribe railway police, but this seems to have become a risky business, espec-ially after the formation of Watch and Ward police detach-ments. Better techniques such as fingerprinting, centralised study of reports, arrest of all possible suspects immediately and simultaneously (so that incriminating stolen goods could not be passed from one gang member to another), all helped. The technique of compelling female suspects to jump around, in the hope that stolen jewelry would drop from those parts of the body where it was secreted, seems to have been more spectacular than infallible.

THE RAILWAY WORKER

By 1903 the Indian railways had over 402,000 employees working on their 30,000 miles of line. Over the next quarter-century the working force doubled, while the mileage increased by one third; in 1929 there were nearly 808,000 employees for 41,000 miles of railway. Labour productivity improved slightly in this period, which saw a doubling of freight traffic and a trebling of passenger. Both the labour force and labour productivity tended to increase in subsequent years.

From the very beginning, when railway construction absorbed workers made available partly by the abolition of slavery in India, the role of the railways as major employers had great social consequences. Not only were they collectively India's biggest employer, but their insistence on Western virtues like precision, punctuality, and planning meant that a pool of labour was created which was familiar with, and did not fear, the demands of industrial technology. For traditionalists this was unwelcome, but many Indian nationalists believed that the political independence which they were seeking would be useless without economic independence, which, it seemed, meant the acceptance of western industrial culture. The railways were the earliest and the biggest teachers of this culture, which brought not only the attitudes of Western employers, but also of western labour; railway trade unions, strikes, health and welfare services all had their inspiration in Western practice even though their form often embraced Indian particularities.

The first railway trade union appears to have been founded in 1897, but it was the few years after World War I that saw the fastest, and not altogether encouraging, development of trade unionism. In a country so divided by religion and caste, so habituated to close family relationships, it was not perhaps surprising that the idea of one organisation to represent all the railway workers did not seem to have much appeal. Admittedly this supposed ideal was not achieved in Britain or North America either, but in India the proliferation of small and mutually hostile unions was so marked that it is hard to say how many railway unions there were at any given time. After 1947 an attempt was made to impose rationality, and in 1950 the Ministry of Railways decided to recognise officially only the strongest or more stable unions. There were 32 of these accounting for about half of the railway labour force. The recognised unions affiliated themselves to one or other of two all-India railwaymen's federations, a move which was certainly in the interest of the Government and probably in that of the nation, but not necessarily in the interest of the railwaymen. The reliance on big Government-recognised federations does not mean that railway trade unionism became a purely bureaucratic and brainwashing organisation, as in some parts of the world.

The first notable railway strikes were those of the EIR and EBR in 1906. On the whole despite notable failures strikes and the possibility of strikes did bring, or accelerate, improvements in pay and conditions. Strikes tended to be long-lasting, possibly because the Indian worker could tolerate deprivation, while boards of directors in London could give free rein to their principles, isolated from any doubts or feelings which would be engendered by on-the-spot experience. In 1921–22, for example, it took three months for the two sides to reach a compromise in the EIR strike. Strikes continued in the inter-war period, and during World War II, when the railways and the British were under great pressure, conditions were ideal for strike action. In fact during the war years there were many strikes, but they were usually of short duration (perhaps because of vigorous administrative reaction). The favourite demand was for a 'living wage' and this slogan was much favoured in the post-independence years.

The population of India was about 324m in 1915. In that year the Indian railways employed 600,000 workers; 8,000 of these were European, 10,000 Anglo-Indian, and 582,000 Indian. The question of Indianisation was still controversial. In 1870 nine-tenths of railway employees were Indian, but none occupied high or responsible positions. They were regarded as unfit as mechanics or locomotive drivers. Europeans were recruited locally for training for these jobs. Many were discharged British soldiers, and not always of good character.

In 1870, however, the Government declared that on State railways all posts would be open to Indians, and Indians began to be employed as shunters and drivers. But by 1910, of the 800-odd higher administrative posts in the State railways, only 47 were held by Indians, and few of these were near the top. The Railway Board made it quite clear that it did not have much confidence in Indians, but in 1915 a Public Services Commission recommended that half the higher appointments should go to Indians. In 1924 on the recommendation of the Acworth Committee, the managing companies agreed to recruit three-quarters of their higher staff from Indians. This process naturally took a long time and Indians tended to be excluded for practical reasons. Since the official language of the railways was English, and its examining and recruiting officers were largely British, a British candidate for a post might have a natural advantage over an Indian (in other words, an exceptionally able Indian and an average Briton had equal chances). All responsible positions, such as those of locomotive men, inspectors, and guards, were obtained only after written examinations conducted in English.

Thus in the 1920s Europeans still tended to occupy the best positions, but it was clear that the situation was changing. Most locomotive drivers were European or Anglo-Indian, assisted by two Indian firemen, but Indian drivers were increasing. Conductor-guards on the best passenger trains were usually British ex-soldiers but Anglo-Indians and Indians preponderated in the slower passenger and in freight trains.

Stationmasters at large stations and important junctions were British or Anglo-Indian, but at smaller stations Indian. All correspondence was conducted in English and the British communities used to tell stories (usually true) of howlers by Indian officials lacking a perfect knowledge of the King's English; like the stationmaster who, in requesting a pay rise, emphasised his family responsibilities '. . . I now have to feed six adults and four adultresses.'

Probably Indians did make mistakes in their language and their activities. It is probably true than Indian stationmasters had few qualms about taking a nap while on duty. But possibly the British, in judging others by their own standards, failed to realise that even though the British invented railways, other peoples were quite capable of running them. In 1947 there were only about 200 British officers left, and they soon retired. Indians were already well established in the highest railway posts and more than one Indian general manager had been knighted. They ran the railways well, carrying on British practices as though they were their own.

The attitude of most British railway officers was neither selfish nor foolish, but was influenced by a social isolation which was self-imposed. All, of course, had chosen to work on Indian railways because of the advantages this service seemed to offer, but they were genuinely interested in Indian advancement and believed rightly that their work was valuable to India. If among themselves they cracked jokes about Indians, at work they usually had friendly relationships with their Indian colleagues and understanding attitudes towards their subordinates. In some big towns they were isolated in special railway quarters. Typically such a settlement would be laid out with streets crossing at right angles. The senior European officers tended to congregate at one end of the settlement, with the lesser ranks ('inferior covenanted staff') at the other. There would usually be an Anglican church, a railway club (open only to senior staff), and a railway 'institute' (open to all senior and middle-grade railwaymen). And naturally a golf course to keep the Scots happy. The advantages of this arrangement were clear. Many Europeans simply could not otherwise have survived Indian conditions, they needed a home from home for physical and psychological reasons. This, however, did not provide much opportunity to hear ideas other than the conventional opinions of their fellow countrymen.

There was a sort of territorial army for Europeans and selected Anglo-Indians. Called officially the Auxiliary Force and unofficially the Volunteers, its railway regiments were more than open to any British railway employee. Anyone who did not join might find himelf in disfavour, and at least some contracts of employment stipulated that the employee would join. That this force, which regularly trained with small arms, was usually closed to Indians, indicated quite clearly its purpose and, incidentally, the long-term instability of the British railwayman's position in India.

THE RESULTS

Throughout their existence the Indian railways have been subject to a continuous stream of enquiries, official and unofficial designed to show whether they were doing their job well and if not, why not. Favourable appraisals of the railways generally include the following observations. The railways were a modernising factor, and were largely responsible for introduction of the telegraph and good postal services. They increased wealth and Government revenue, facilitated famine relief and gave market access to the new irrigation settlements. Because they needed timber, the Government forestry service had to be created. For similar reasons the Government had to establish its own engineering and survey departments. In such ways the railways brought about the end of laissez-faire in India. They also provided new employment, especially for the humbler classes, and their creation of a new artisan class transformed society.

The population became more mobile. By 1914 the average Indian made 1.4 journeys each year, compared with the 1.2 of the average Russian and the 27 of the average Briton. Travel helped to break down barriers of caste as well as of distance. Pilgrimage became possible for greater numbers of people. A popular travel book, *India of the Queen*, observed: 'The chances of a god doing a large and increasing business are greatly improved by a railway station. Juggernaut himself, after defying the calumnies of a century, now finds his popularity imperilled for want of railway communication.' (In 1897 the BNR rescued Juggernaut with a branch line). On the freight side, the railways reduced the cost of commodities; for example, the price of salt in Nagpur was halved when the railway link with Bombay was completed. In 1846–56 Indian cotton exports doubled, and imports of manufactures more than doubled. Whole areas, which could rely on the railways for delivery of grain, were able to concentrate their production on industrial crops; the Central Provinces concentrated on cotton, Bengal on jute. The needs of the railways stimulated the opening of new coal mines, including several in areas not previously exploited. The new economic interdependence between regions was one of several factors fostering national unity. In other ways the railways encouraged, or imposed, unity. An agreed standardisation of that variable measure of weight, the maund, was achieved. 'Railway time' was the first step in instituting a standard time for India (and, incidentally, from the early days the railways used the 24hr clock). Customs and excise duties at the boundaries of provinces and States were, from 1868, collected at the place of origin so that trains no longer needed to halt for inspection at boundaries. The railways, needing reliable feeder services, encouraged road programmes, and all-the-year-round local road services.

More critical commentators blame the railways for the increased export of food products, much of which could have been consumed in India. The railways' encouragement of the import trade meant the ruin of the Indian handicraft industry, a social disaster comparable with the enclosure movement in 18th-century Britain. 'Interdependence' is only a euphemism for the breakdown of that local self-sufficiency on which India society was traditionally based.

As for the so-called famine railways, it was said that these merely absorbed funds which could have been used for further irrigation projects. Irrigation was a far better investment in terms of famine relief. Railway tariff policies discouraged industrialisation and the railways' encouragement of industrialisation simply meant the spread of inhuman factory conditions and the disappearance of conventional morality (the confusion of this last sentence reflects a similar confusion in the writings of several of the critics). Above all, the railways were a severe drain on the resources of the Indian taxpayer, who all too often suffered for the benefit of foreign capitalists.

This last question, of the financial burden posed by the railways, was always a hot issue. Whether or not the Government gained or lost from its various financial involvements in both State and private lines was largely a question of how the figures were chosen. But it is probably fair to say that until the turn of the century, taking the average of good and bad periods, the Government paid out more than it received. In the 20th century, however, this situation was reversed, so that by the 1940s there was probably an even balance. Paradoxically, though not unexpectedly, the most profitable years were those in which public complaints were loudest: in the war years.

In World War 1 increasing traffic and railway under-capacity meant dissatisfaction for passengers and consignors, but also an intensive use of assets so that in the best year (1918) net earnings were eight per cent of estimated capital investment. During World War II the railways had even greater tasks and problems. They had just passed through a decade of depression in which net earnings fell (in 1932) to around 3 per cent of capital and then, in 1941, were faced with an invasion threat and virtual isolation from Britain. Isolation from Europe meant that India had quickly to establish new industries to supply both herself and the allied war effort in southern Asia. From time to time nationalists enthusiastically sabotaged railway communications. About 1000 miles of branch lines were dismantled, and some mg locomotives withdrawn, in order to assemble railway equipment for the war zones, including East Africa and the Middle East. Meanwhile there were large-scale troop movements, not only of incoming European troops, but of the 2.5m strong Indian army (all volunteers) which had been recruited. With all the extra traffic, net earnings rose in the final two years of war to almost 10 per cent of capital, only to fall by half in the first postwar year, and by almost half again in the second.

Discussion of the effects of Indian railway building during

Page 87 (above) WG 2–8–2 with a crew rest car behind the tender, on the CR near Agra in 1963; (below) Indian Railways' last steam design, a WL light Pacific at Kankariya shed (WR) in 1972

Page 88 (above) Hyderabad–Manmad train leaving Aurangabad in 1963, on the former Nizam's State Railway metre-gauge line, hauled by a YP Pacific; (below) metre gauge locomotives at Sabarmati (WR) in 1972. From left to right: Ajmer-built D 4–6–4T, YB Pacific, YL 2–6–2, and a 4–6–0 (coaling)

the Imperial years would not be complete without reference to the influence which Indian experience had on railway building in other parts of the British Empire. Burma, which was not separated, administratively, from India until 1937, had 2,060 miles of mg railway by that year, built to Indian standards and style. The short-lived 29-mile mg Aden Railway, was also an Indian affair, but perhaps the most notable 'Indian' railway abroad was the East African system. When, in the 1890s, construction began of the Mombasa–Lake Victoria line in Britain's newly acquired East African territory, Indian labour and Indian experience were employed. Partly this was because India was often regarded as the Empire's standard-setter; what had proved good in India should be good enough for Africa. Partly it was because the British, unlike the Germans in neighbouring Tanganyika, distrusted the ability of Africans to build or operate railways. And partly it was a feeling that a standardisation between Indian and East African railway practice was strategically desirable (as indeed proved to be the case in 1941). Thus the first surveys for the new line were carried out by a party sent from India and composed predominantly of Indians. About 32,000 Indian labourers were imported to build the line, of whom 2500 died during construction. Nearly a quarter of the survivors settled in Kenya and Uganda when the railway was built. Until World War II, the General Managers of the East African Railways were former Indian railway officers. Many of the locomotives were imported second-hand from India, or built to Indian design; the standard 4–8–0 introduced in 1915 was of a design originated on the Assam Bengal Railway.

CHAPTER THREE

After Independence

PARTITION AND AFTER

BRITAIN'S Indian Empire came to an end on 15 August 1947, being replaced by the new nations of India and Pakistan. Months before the transfer of power, animosity between Moslems and Hindus, aggravated by the political events of the day, was taking violent forms. Violence came to a head after independence, and the railways were among the main sufferers. The worst area was the Punjab, where the boundary between India and West Pakistan passed through, and thus divided, the traditional homeland of the Sikhs. There were disturbances around Lahore before 15 August, but train services remained normal until mid-August. Trains across the new frontier were temporarily halted on 20 August, and elsewhere services were curtailed because coal trains were held up. By late September, the skeleton services operated in the Punjab had to be abandoned, so as to allow the railways to deal with the refugee problem. Hindus were fleeing for their lives from Pakistan; Moslems were in turn fleeing for their lives from India. Floods in late September cut two main lines, making things worse.

On 24 August the Frontier Mail arrived one day late at Bombay. En route it had been held up by about 200 armed men. Baggage had been looted, the train had been searched, and some passengers murdered. Other less celebrated trains received the same treatment. Around Lahore, because of the communal murders, railway staff instead of reporting for duty stayed at home to protect their families. Those train crews still at work refused to cross the border. For some weeks only a couple of freight trains and the Frontier Mail crossed the Indo-Pakistani border, which cut what had once been the NWR's busy main line between Amritsar and Lahore. Soon even these trains ceased running. Passenger trains which formerly had run to Lahore and beyond terminated at Delhi, although after December most were extended to Amritsar, which later became their permanent terminus.

As millions of refugees took to the roads and railways, the stations became crowded with people awaiting special refugee trains. These crowds were a convenient target for religious activists. As in the country at large, every possible crime and atrocity was perpetrated in this period. In the stations jam-packed with insanitary humanity, corpses lay for days un-attended. In the trains alarm chains would be pulled at pre-arranged spots, so that passengers could be murdered at leisure in lineside ambushes. Near Amritsar a train of Moslem refugees was attacked in September, and about 3000 passengers butch-ered. As a reprisal (so it was said, but it would probably have happened anyway), a train containing Hindu and Sikh passen-gers was ambushed some days later near Lahore, and about 1500 passengers were killed. It became the practice for each refugee train (typically carrying about 5000 passengers) to be provided with an escort of 60 soldiers, travelling at the rear of the train in a sandbagged flat wagon, armed with a Bren gun. This was not always sufficient, however; while the troops were safe in their mobile earthwork, passengers in the front of the train were virtually unprotected. Moreover as else-where, troops tended to identify themselves with their co-religionists, even after the death penalty was introduced to punish soldiers failing to make proper efforts to protect life and property.

From mid-August to mid-September alone, the railways handled about 700,000 refugees, despite their own difficulties of staffing and congestion. At Bombay both termini were encumbered by thousands of Moslems awaiting transport to Pakistan. In Delhi hordes of Hindu refugees settled in the stations and also in Moslem holy places, resulting in riots and a very ugly situation as the remaining Moslems began to be murdered. All lines out of Delhi were closed for a week. Towards the end of 1947, however, the situation calmed. Even the mg Delhi–Ahmedabad line, which had been closed for three months, was able to resume operations.

There was a new clash in January 1948. A train of Hindu refugees drew into a station crowded with Moslems who thought that this was the train which they had been awaiting for several days. When the Moslems tried to enter the train, its escort, unnerved, threw a grenade. This attracted the attention of some passing tribesmen who, unable to let pass such a temptation, opened fire. There were about 1000 casualties before Pakistani troops put an end to the carnage. In these conditions accidents, unless a result of a removed rail and the prelude to something worse, were regarded as only minor irritants. At Sambhu 171 refugees died in a derailment. At Jullundur a refugee, one of hundreds travelling on the carriage roof, let fall his metal trunk between two coaches and the result was a derailment with 24 deaths.

Among the refugees were of course railwaymen. This loss of staff caused great difficulties during subsequent years, not least because Moslems, many of whom fled to Pakistan, traditionally supplied a disproportionate number of locomotive men, while the Hindus, many of whom fled to India from Pakistan, tended to concentrate on traffic, clerical and signalling work. Geographically the damaging effect of Partition on the railways was unmistakable. British policy in India has sometimes been described as divide and rule, but certainly the railway system had made no divisive distinctions This meant that the network was unsuited to the division resulting from Partition. The NWR in the west and the BAR in the east were split arbitrarily, and took years to recover. Of the NWR's 6881 miles, only 1885 came to India, forming an essential but hardly viable unit known as the Eastern Punjab Railway. The Bengal–

Assam Railway, with bg and mg mileages, consisted of 3555 miles on the eve of Partition, of which 1942 were in Indian territory after independence. This Indian mileage was divided between the EIR, the Oudh–Tirhut Railway and a new Assam Railway. Elsewhere, the mg Jodhpur Railway lost the 319 miles which entered West Pakistan. Deteriorating political relations between India and Pakistan aggravated the difficulties of Partition. The NWR in West Pakistan, which became the Pakistan Western Railway, was deprived of Indian coal and was obliged to convert its locomotives to oil burning. The original hope that mg workshops, situated in East Pakistan, would continue to handle repairs for India's Assam Railway, and that the EIR would handle bg repairs for East Pakistan's bg lines, came to nothing.

REORGANISATION

Regroupings of Indian railways had been seriously considered ever since the 1920s, when 'Grouping' of the British railways in 1923 had seemed to show the way. Most advantages of such re-grouping (standardisation, pooling of rolling stock, uniform tariffs) had already been obtained through the co-ordinating functions of the Railway Board. By 1944 company-managed and company-owned lines were eliminated, with a few very minor exceptions, and uniform pay scales were achieved in the same year, but the unsatisfactory situation resulting from Partition, with the incorporation of the Princely States (with their railways), made a reorganisation imperative. This took the form of a division of the Indian railway system into what were officially called 'zonal administrative units', more commonly known simply as railways (see maps on pages 181-185). The first to be formed was the Southern Railway in April 1951. This railway comprised 6000 miles, being the amalgamation of the Madras & Southern Mahratta, South Indian, and Mysore State railways.

In the following November the Central Railway was formed by amalgamating the GIP and the Nizam's State Railway, and adding the smaller Scindia and Dholpur State railways, making a total of 5400 miles. Simultaneously the GIP's old rival, the BBCI, became the Western Railway, which also absorbed the mg State railways in the territory (the Saurashtra, Jaipur State, Rajasthan State, and Cutch State railways, and part of the Jodhpur Railway) making a total of 5460 miles.

In April 1952 the remaining railways were regrouped. The Northern Railway, of 6000 miles, comprised the Eastern Punjab Railway (India's share of the old NWR), most of the Jodhpur Railway, the Bikaner State Railway, the Delhi–Fazilka section of the Western Railway's mg line from Ahmedabad, and those sections of the EIR east of Moghal Sarai. The remainder of the EIR was amalgamated with the BNR to form the Eastern Railway, with 5700 miles. Finally the mg lines north of the Ganges, with the Kanpur (Cawnpore)–Achnera mg section of the Western Railway, were amalgamated to form the North Eastern Railway (4800 miles). Thus there had come into being six major Government-owned, Government-managed, railways totalling nearly 34,000 route-miles. These railways also operated about 350 miles of branch lines owned by district boards or small companies.

There remained the harbour railways, and 14 small non-Government railways operating 553 miles of narrow-gauge line. The most important of the latter were three short lines managed by Messrs McLeod and subsequently taken over by the Government, and the Martin railways. Martin & Company operated two suburban lines from Howrah, two lines near Patna (the Arrah–Sasaram and the Futwah–Islampur light railways), and a substantial line near Delhi, the Shahdara–Saharanpur Railway. After labour disturbances, the two Howrah lines were closed, but it seemed recently that they might be taken over by the West Bengal Government.

In creating the new zonal railways, the aim had been systems serving compact areas, big enough to maintain their own full-scale administrations and workshops. As time passed, it seemed that some of the new railways were too big, and changes were made. In 1957 the Eastern Railway was divided.

What were formerly the BNR lines were detached to form the South Eastern Railway, the remainder continuing as the Eastern Railway. In 1958, because of the special strategic and geographic circumstances of Assam, the lines serving that region were detached from the North Eastern Railway, becoming the Northeast Frontier Railway (NFR). In 1965 two divisions of the Central Railway and the two most prosperous divisions of the Southern Railway were detached and amalgamated to form the new South Central Railway, with headquarters at Secunderabad (the old headquarters of the Nizam's State Railway). This new creation has been variously described as 'a response to public opinion' and 'a purely political move'. Both descriptions add up to the same thing, perhaps; but the creation of new railway zones remains a controversial subject. Local public opinion presses for the creation of new, more local, railway zones; and certainly the more railway zones there are, the more jobs for the boys can be found. There does come a time when a given railway is so big and busy that it loses touch with its clients. But the creation of the SCR weakened the CR and SR, while giving birth to a railway which was barely big enough to be really independent and which did not (for example) possess enough workshop capacity to repair its locomotives.

From the mid-1950s all railways were organised on the divisional rather than the departmental principle. It was under the respective Divisional Superintendents that co-ordination between the various departments was achieved, not at headquarters. Hitherto, some railways had favoured one structure, and others another. In the 1920s the NWR and EIR had become divisional, while the GIP was peculiar in that its operating, running and mechanical sectors were organised divisionally, and the other sectors departmentally.

The managements of each railway enjoy some degree of independence as can be seen, for example, in the different locomotive liveries of the various railways, and in the different facilities which they offer, but they are subject to the Railway Board in Delhi. The Railway Board, which is really a ministry, is headed by a cabinet minister, assisted by a deputy. Apart from its function as a ministry (planning, building, maintenance and operation) it also acts as an executive headquarters for the day-to-day running of the railways and for setting technical standards. It consists of five members. Since the departure of the British there has been a tendency for political influence to predominate more frequently over bureaucratic. Appointment of politicians as railway ministers has both symbolised and assisted this tendency. Sometimes the results have been bad; most railwaymen seem to feel that political influence, especially the influence of local politicians, has sometimes led to wrong decisions. On the other hand, bureaucratic convenience, the placing of efficiency before all else, has its own perils. Parliamentary control is exercised, or can be exercised, in the annual debate on the Railway Budget and by raising complaints at other times; in some years as many as one-tenth of Parliamentary questions have been devoted to railway matters. The number of effective questions, however, is much fewer; most seem to be requests by members for local benefits which cannot immediately be granted (better train service, conversion to bg, and so on). Members of Parliament also sit on the National and Zonal Railway Users' Consultative Councils, which are supposed to protect the interests of railway users. How effective these bodies are is difficult to judge. They certainly act as safety valves, and help to keep the railway administrations in touch with public opinion, but they can hardly initiate action. Their members are appointed, not elected.

NEW CONSTRUCTION

Having to share Government investment funds with the rest of the economy, and already possessing a network dense by the standards of other developing nations, the Indian railways did not indulge in any spectacular railway building in the first Five-Year plans. What resources they had for development were devoted to the construction of short lines serving particular industries or relieving bottlenecks, to double-tracking key sections and, in a few cases, to converting mg trackage to bg. In 1951 there were about 33,300 route miles of track. Of these, broad, metre, and narrow gauge accounted respectively for 15,700, 15,000 and 2600 miles. In 1971 the total had grown to 37,000 miles, divided between the gauges thus: 18,000, 16,000, and 3000 miles. Thus the bg, which produced 84 per cent of the tonne-km and 72 per cent of the passenger-km, comprised almost half of the total mileage. By 1971 6645 miles of the bg routes were double track, including 240 miles of multiple-track. On the mg, 273 miles were double, while the narrow gauge was single throughout.

On the Eastern and South Eastern railways there were a number of new bg lines built to ease transport of coal and of raw materials for the new steel plants. The most important of these was the 183-mile link from Chandrapura to Muri and Bondamunda, opened in 1964. To relieve the heavily loaded lines to the west through Moghal Sarai, and at the same time to develop the Singrauli coalfield, a 158-mile line was laid eastwards from Katni on the Central Railway, linking up in 1972 with the Eastern Railway. Perhaps the most ambitious of the new lines was the so-called DBK project. This comprised three lines, totalling 423 miles, to ease the export of ores through Vishakhapatnam. One of the three lines (Kottavalasa-Kirandul), passing through the Eastern Ghats, included 45 continuous miles of 1 in 64 grades, 61 tunnels, and 1,300 bridges. 3,200-ton ore trains are planned on this section; two diesel locomotives are needed to haul the empties up the Ghats, and three to control the loaded trains downhill.

On the other side of India, another line to facilitate ore exports was the Southern Railway's mg link between Hassan and the port of Mangalore. This was expected to be finished in 1974. Mangalore was already served by a bg line, and the new mg route was to provide a shorter trip and avoid transhipment; however, bridges and tunnels are built to bg standards in anticipation of subsequent gauge conversion. Another mg line built for the SR was that between Bangalore and Salem. Both terminals of this line had bg and mg connections, but mg was adopted so as to make a practical mg route to the far South. A proposed bg route from the southern tip of India up to Delhi and the Himalayas also concerned the SR. Although this route was to mainly comprise existing trackage, it did involve some new construction around Trivandrum, besides conversion to bg of certain mg lines.

Yet another port whose development was aided by railway construction was Kandla, the most northerly port on the west coast of the Republic of India. Its existing mg connection was supplemented by a new 144-mile bg branch of the Western Railway from Jhund (near Viramgam). Other new lines on the WR included the mg Udaipur–Himmatnagar line of 132 miles, and the 120 mile Guna–Maksi line. The latter was intended to open up isolated territory and provide an alternative route for coal traffic from the east.

Bombay and the area in and around Delhi received avoiding lines, to relieve congestion. At Delhi, pressure on the existing junctions was relieved by a number of short lines, enabling a new marshalling yard to be built at Tughlakabad, 12 miles to the south. In Bombay, the Central Railway operated a new 43 mile avoiding line from Diva to Apta. There were proposals to built a long new line down the west coast from Apta to Mangalore.

On the NER, almost entirely mg, new construction was confined to short relieving works. However a number of these were significant. In particular, when barrage schemes enabled lines to cross rivers, inefficient transhipment by train ferry was eliminated. A possible bg line from Raxaul into Nepal was under study in 1972.

On the Northern Railway the most significant development was connected with the dispute with Pakistan over Jammu and Kashmir. Initially, India's rail link with this territory ended at Pathankot, but a line was built from Pathankot to Jammu. Continuation into Kashmir seemed doubtful, however, because of the forbidding terrain. But there was a proposal, seriously studied, to build a mg railway in the Vale of Kashmir It was thought that such a line, though isolated, could be viable if it made use of hydro-electricity.

Tension with Pakistan was felt also in NE India. The formation of East Pakistan meant that the previous route from Calcutta into Assam fell out of Indian control. To provide an all-Indian rail link, a mg route was developed in 1948. The Haldibari–New Jalpaiguri section of this probably holds the world record for gauge conversion. When originally laid, in British India, it was mg because that gauge was accepted as the standard north of the Ganges. It was later converted to bg when a new bridge over the Ganges at Sara provided the opportunity for an all-bg route from Calcutta to New Jalpaiguri. Reconverted to mg in 1948, it was widened again in 1966 in common with the rest of the route. In 1971, when the Farakka Bridge was opened, it became possible to travel from Calcutta to New Jalpaiguri by bg throughout. This route, with the mg continuation into Assam, is a line of great strategic significance. It conveys tea (a principle earner of scarce foreign exchange) and Assam's small but important output of oil. It supplies areas which are particularly sensitive (the rebellious Nagaland, frontiers with China and Pakistan) and is very much subject to sabotage. In two wars against Pakistan and one against China it carried the bulk of military traffic. The most successful of these wars, the Bangladesh campaign of 1971, began immediately after the opening of the Farrakka Bridge, which removed the most serious bottleneck.

Policy since 1947 regarding gauges has always been based on the intention eventually to convert all lines, except perhaps a few in difficult country, to bg. In practice, financial limitations permitted only the most urgent conversions. For populations (and especially politicians) of the mg areas, this remains a live issue. What is surprising, perhaps, is not the number and intensity of the campaigns launched to persuade the Railway Ministry to widen particular mg lines, but the general failure of such campaigns. This phenomenon of the Railway Ministry, apparently besieged by political and popular pressures, steadfastly but unobtrusively refusing to budge from its plans, has been evident in other railway matters, and seems to suggest that at this early period of Indian democracy the experts (or bureaucrats) have not suffered from political pressures quite as much as they sometimes claim. Possibly the electoral dominance of the ruling political party strengthened the hand of successive Railway Ministers.

In the 1950s and 1960s the mg in fact strengthened its hold. When new lines had to be built in mg areas, they were naturally themselves mg. This is why, despite some widenings, the mg mileage continued to increase. Moreover, the Central Railway's new mg line from Khandwa to Purna provided a link between the Southern Railway's mg system and the rest of India. With the opening of the bridge over the Brahmaputra in Assam in 1963 it became technically feasible (though economically impractical) to send a mg wagon from the NE frontier terminus at Ledo to the southern tip of India at Trivandrum. In the 1970s, however, considerable inroads into mg mileage were made or proposed. The first large-scale conversion was the former M & SM main line southwards from Poona. Relaying to bg was completed as far as Miraj and Kolhapur in 1971. On the Southern Railway, conversion of the Bangalore–Guntakal section was under way in 1972; the Trivandrum–Ernakulam, Bangalore–Mysore, Bangalore–Hubli sections, and the Guntakal–Secunderabad line of the SCR were likely to follow. On the NER, 355 miles of main line between Barabanki and Samastipur were under consideration; the NER's first short length of bg route had already been achieved, with the conversion of the Samastipur–Barauni line (connecting via the new Mokameh Bridge over the Ganges with the ER bg main line south of that river). On the Western Railway an important conversion was begun in 1972: the 346-mile Viramgam–Okha–Porbandar line. Conversion of this to bg was expected greatly to benefit the economic development of that part of Gujarat, as well as eliminate much costly transhipment at Viramgam. As for the very busy mg main line from Ahmedabad to Delhi, conversion of this is likely, for it was under study in 1972.

THE RAILWAY WORKER

Indian railways employed 914,000 men and women in 1951,

and this grew steadily to 1,373,000 in 1971. Since railway traffic increased faster than this, labour productivity rose during the period and seemed likely to continue doing so, despite the general policy that modernisation should not cause any redundancy. About one-fifth of the labour force in the early 1970s was casual, hired mainly for construction work and not enjoying all the advantages of the regular workers, such as job security.

Formally, staff recruitment was devised to preclude nepotism, parochialism, favouritism and corruption. In practice, it is hard to say how far this object was achieved. Unskilled workers were recruited by local committees, and vacancies were widely advertised. Higher staff were selected by Railway Service Commissions, while the most senior officers ('gazetted staff') were selected by the Government Public Service Commission. Written examination were still a prerequisite for the more responsible jobs; aspiring locomotive men still sat for examinations set by Cambridge University. In the early 1950s it was decided that literacy should be required of all employees. How far or fast this intention has been achieved is, again, uncertain, but the railways did provide incentives and opportunities for their staff to attend literacy classes.

The question of literacy was inseparable from India's controversial linguistic problem. With a majority of the population speaking Hindi, it was inevitable that leaders from the traditional Hindi-speaking areas should urge adoption of Hindi as the national language. This was resisted in other parts, especially in the South, which regarded language barriers as a safeguard against dominance by other regions of India. In the early 1950s the SR was the only railway which did not publish a Hindi version of its timetable. Rather than let Hindi replace English as the *lingua franca* of India, public opinion in South India preferred English, not entirely without reason either. For example, in competitive examinations held in English every candidate irrespective of his mother tongue would be equal, whereas in a Hindi-language examination the non-Hindi linguistic groups would be at a disadvantage. Nevertheless,

Hindi seemed likely to triumph eventually. By the later 1950s the SR was publishing its timetable in eleven languages, including Hindi. Hindi scholars, as part of an attempt to make their language fit for modern use, worked out Hindi equivalents for railway terms more convenient than the time-honoured makeshifts like *Chariot of fire*. In 1956 it became obligatory for staff passing out of railway training schools to pass an elementary Hindi examination. In 1961 all but the older railwaymen were instructed to attend classes. Station nameboards gave Hindi, English and (where appropriate) the local language variants. A number of placenames were Hindified. In the early 1970s, for example, Baroda became Vadodara and Poona Pune, following the earlier example of Varanasi (Benares).

Being the largest employer and a Government employer, the railways must set an example. Thus they are generous in the amenities provided for employees. By the end of the 1960s, they provided more than 500,000 housing units, besides schools for railwaymen's children, medical and hospital services (beyond the means of the ordinary Indian), cheap foodshops and canteens, and recreation facilities (under the auspices of railway institutes). They observe as best they can the Government's insistence that a proportion of the better jobs must be reserved for the 'scheduled castes' ('Untouchables'). From time to time pay commissions have awarded increased wage rates, although these are not always received with great joy. Strikes occur, as do protest fasts and refusals to accept pay packets regarded as too small.

Although in 1953, with the regrouping of railways, the two main federations of Indian railway trade unions combined, by the 1970s it seemed that there might again be an inefficient proliferation of unions. By then the railways dealt mainly with two federations, but inside those federations specialist craft unions were multiplying. There were over 700 categories of employees on the railways, and many categories or groups of categories have formed their own unions in the hope of receiving more attention for their demands. This has caused inter-union tension, with each seeking to show itself more militant than its rivals. Union office-holders, in the Indian tradition, do not need to be employees and are often political figures.

Although on large issues of policy the personal influence of politicians has remained small, in staff matters it could be all-important. It was suggested at one stage by a reputable committee of inquiry that the Railway Ministry should regularly table for public scrutiny all letters received from members of Parliament on behalf of individual employees. Only thus could the country know how large, or how little, was the effect of political patronage on appointment and promotion. In many places the local party boss of the ruling party is all-powerful. Not only can he obtain scarce passenger accomodation reservations or get wagons placed for the party faithful and their friends but he can, it is alleged, arrange the dismissal of railway employees who refuse to play his game. Another damaging influence on the railwaymens' morale are probably the highly-praised 'vigilance organisations'. These were set up in railway establishments to detect irregularities and corruption. In practice, although they have procured some arrests and have undoubtedly deterred many potential miscreants, they sometimes create an atmosphere of inquisition, false accusation and spying.

For locomotive drivers the retiring age is 55, extendable to 58. Those needing spectacles are provided with two pairs, for which they sign each time they go on duty. Their pay includes a basic wage plus mileage allowance. Many locomotive depots operate a one-engine-one-crew system; in such cases the names of the regular driver, fireman, and assistant are shown on the side of the cab. Elsewhere locomotives are pooled or, sometimes, shared between two crews. On the Central Railway, for example, when traction sections are long (over $9\frac{1}{2}$ hr) one crew rides in a first class compartment and takes over halfway. For the same purpose on freight trains, the CR introduced crew rest cars, usually a modified coach next to the locomotive. But locomotive men then demanded, it is said, regular changes of linen and travelling cooks, accordingly the idea was dropped on the CR, although it survives on other railways. Also likely to survive for some years is the third man in the cab of steam locomotives. Mechanical stokers are not favoured, and the assistant is very much needed at least on the larger engines. In the 1920s the BNR abolished the third man, but soon restored him after locomotive crews paralysed the system by bringing in their trains hours behind schedule, claiming that they had run short of steam.

FREIGHT TRAFFIC

Nehru, India's first prime minister, intended to raise the standard of living, eliminate poverty and improve production per head to approach that of the developed nations. At the same time he proposed to revise traditional Hindu social norms, so that, for example, the rights of the individual in India would be as extensive as those in Western democracies. Each of these objectives, economic and social, would alone have been daunting; to achieve both simultaneously seemed to many quite impossible. In retrospect, it would seem that although there were many failures, although India today in some respects does not resemble the India which Nehru was trying to build, in general a peaceful revolution has been accomplished.

For the railways, both the economic and social changes have had great significance. The freeing of women and Untouchables from repressive Hindu social laws, for example, has entailed important changes in staff recruitment. Concern for the poor meant great changes in third class passenger services. Above all, rapid and planned economic development mean that the first care of the railways is to ensure that the increased demand for freight services is met. The planned economy could not work if transport were restricted by bottlenecks. The National Planning Commission was established in 1950, just as the economy was returning to normal after Partition, and the first Indian Five-Year plan followed, covering 1950–51 to 1955–56. The results of this and subsequent five-year plans can be seen in the figures of freight handled by the railways.

Page 105 (above) SR metre gauge locomotives at Bangalore City (SR) in 1963. On the left is an old F class 0–6–0 and on the right a post-war YL 2–6–2; (below) an F class 0–6–0 comes to grief at Bangalore (1963)

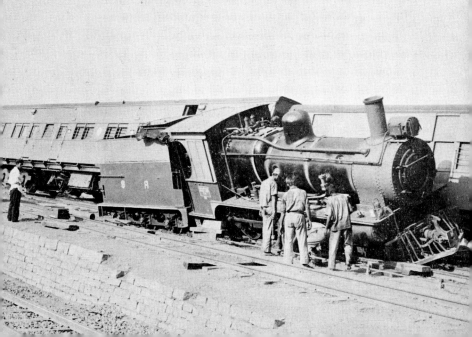

Page 106 (above) A WDM2 diesel passes Ahmedabad station with a load of grain in open box wagons. The photograph was taken in 1972, when electrification was in progress; *(below)* the metre gauge Delhi Express leaves Ahmedabad behind a Canadian-built YDM4 diesel

In 1950–51 the railways carried 93m tonnes of freight, in 1960–61 156m, and in 1970–71 196m. Largely because road transport took much of the short-distance traffic during those 21 years, the average length of haul for freight traffic rose from 294 miles to 403 miles. Thus tonne-miles increased even more than tonnage.

The most important single traffic remained coal; 64m tonnes was moved in 1970–71, of which 16million was for the railways' own use. The development during the plans of State metallurgical centres meant that the iron and steel industry became the second greatest source of freight traffic. In 1970–71 raw materials (excluding coal) destined for the steel plants amounted to 16m tonnes, while finished products from those plants contributed 7m tonnes. In addition, iron and manganese ores moved to ports for export totalled 11m tonnes. Food-grains accounted for 15m tonnes, cement for 11m and railway materials (including ballast) for 16m.

Coal is by far the most important fuel in India; Hydro-electric sources of energy have still to be fully exploited, while most oil has to be imported. Apart from providing the railways with one-third of their freight traffic, coal is the product on which planned economic development is most dependent. Unfortunately, although coal reserves are abundant, they are not well situated. Although there are deposits in Central India and elsewhere, four-fifths of the coal is mined in the east in Bengal and Bihar. About one-third of this coal is consumed locally, in Calcutta and the coalfield districts, which means that two-thirds is despatched to distant destinations. In particular, in Western India the industries of the Bombay and Ahmedabad regions are largely dependent on eastern coal. Taking the western region alone, about one-quarter of India's energy resources are consumed in this one region, whose industries are 750–950 miles from the coalfields. To ensure the maintenance of coal supplies in the face of rapidly increasing consumption the railways have had to evolve special techniques and make special investments. Despite these, towards the end of the 1950s there were signs of an impending transport crisis. This was averted, but by the early

1970s there were further difficulties arising from a freight car shortage.

The line with the highest traffic density in India is the Eastern Railway's main route from Asansol, serving the coalfields, to Moghal Sarai, near Benares. Along this route moves coal for North and Central India, besides much for Western India. This was the first main line to be dieselised and later, when dieselisation proved insufficient, it was electrified. Other measures were the introduction of new four-axle high-capacity wagons which afford greater payload for a given train length, the operation of block trains, consisting entirely of coal wagons from a single source to a single destination, and the encouragement by tariff adjustments of rail/sea shipments to Western India via the port of Calcutta.

Meanwhile, double-tracking, loop-lengthening, re-signalling and other measures have been taken to relieve the more hard-pressed lines between the coalfields and the rest of India. The block train, which could weigh 3600 tons compared with the 2200 tons of conventional trains of the same length has been the single most important of these innovations. Not only are the block trains heavier, but they also move faster, averaging 200–250 miles per day. By 1970–71 two-thirds of coal movements was by block train.

To ensure that the smaller users of coal could be served by block trains, the railways arranged to help establish coal dumps in the areas of demand. These dumps would be organised by local authorities. They would be supplied by block trains and would distribute the coal in small lots to the local consumers. This seemed a very logical arrangement, but progress has been slow. The railways built special sidings. and made land available, but the coal dumps often failed to materialise. Probably lack of co-operation on the part of local Governments was the cause of this. Another useful policy which was rather slow to get under way was the building of power stations near the collieries; this was to enable part of the energy requirements to be despatched to consuming areas by high tension wires instead of by freight train.

A World Bank study in the early 1960s commended the Indian railways for their handling of coal traffic, reporting that although locomotives and signalling were old-fashioned, the line capacity was so intensively used that operating indices compared quite favourably with those of the more developed countries. The difficulties which were beginning to accumulate in the early 1970s largely centre round the non-supply of empties for loading. This has been partly a result of the disturbed social and political circumstances of Eastern India, partly of coal production developing in ways not anticipated by the plans, and (according to the railways) partly of the failure of many large mines to instal planned mechanical loading facilities and of consumers to unload their wagons promptly.

Block trains were increasingly used for bulk freight other than coal. However, the haulage of more and more freight did not improve the financial position of the railways, due to tariff peculiarities. After 1947 the use of tapering tariffs became more common. The longer the haul, the cheaper the rate per mile. This has had the effect, among others, that coal moving more than 340 miles did so at a loss; only up to that distance were costs covered by revenue. Railway tariffs, moreover, both passenger and freight, have increased much more slowly than labour costs, fuel and material prices.

Studies in the early 1970s showed that eleven major commodities were carried at a loss. Some of these were not surprising (manure, grass, firewood, sugar cane) but others were significant (export ores, unpressed cotton). In addition, on the less efficient mg system there were other unprofitable traffics, including such staples as foodgrains, ores, limestone, coal and fertilisers. In all, about 40 per cent of tonnage moved was unprofitable, either because of low tariffs or because of tapering tariffs.

Partly as a result of this, partly because industrial production fell unexpectedly behind its planned increase, the railways, which had hitherto been profitable, were in deficit from 1966–67, although it was hoped that by 1972 a surplus would once again be achieved. Gross receipts always covered working expenses (including depreciation), but the net revenue remaining did not suffice to cover the 6 per cent 'dividend' payable to the General Exchequer as interest on capital. Optimism about a surplus in 1972 was based on some tariff increases sanctioned by a reluctant Parliament to bring rates closer to (but not abreast of) current wage and price levels, and a reduction of dividend liability on capital invested in lines kept open for strategic or social reasons.

Political considerations prevented the railways raising freight and passenger rates as much as they wished; even with the new rates, coal traffic was still unprofitable over distances greater than 560 miles. In effect this and other similar phenomena represented the subsidisation by other railway users of certain industries, more particularly those industries located far from their raw materials.

While the railways were gaining bulk traffic, largely unprofitable, they were losing the more highly rated traffic to road competition. As elsewhere in the world, the lorry owner, apart from offering door-to-door transport, is free to pick and choose his traffic. At first, the diversion to the roads of traffic, especially non-bulk traffic, was not unwelcome, because in the first two Five-Year plans the main anxiety of the railways was not revenue, but finding capacity to satisfy demand.

However, when deficits began to appear the higher-rated traffic seemed more desirable, and efforts were made to regain it. In 1970, the managers of the respective railways were given the power to offer selected clients virtually unlimited reductions on the normal rates, so as to compete with road rates (previously, managers could not offer more than a 25 per cent reduction). About the same time, like other railways facing road competition, the Indian railways realised that they had little idea of how much the various traffics actually cost to move. More attention was paid to cost studies, so that rates for specific flows could be quoted which were both competitive and profitable.

It also began to be realised that road transport won traffic not simply through low rates, but through quality of service. This realisation led to the introduction of regular fast freight services between major centres, and finally to containerisation. Fast freight services were introduced by several railways in 1965, but did not win a high rate of patronage. The Western Railway's Ahmedabad Arrow, for example, at first ran the 306 miles from Bombay to Ahmedabad daily, but within a few months was reduced to a tri-weekly service. Goods were accepted at origin up to 16.00, and were delivered at destination the next day from 14.00. Traffic documents (invoices etc.) were carried by the guard, so that consignees could take delivery immediately on arrival. Other transits by fast freights in the mid-1960s were 22hr by the Southern Railway's 220 mile Madras–Bangalore service, 99hr by the CR/SER Bombay–Howrah service, and the five-day transit of the NR/ER New Delhi–Howrah service.

By 1972 the fast freight schedules were improved somewhat, but traffic by then was still disappointing. The Bombay–Calcutta service was down to 86hr but still ran only bi-weekly, although the New Delhi–Howrah service had become a daily, on a 72hr timing. In that year such trains (known as 'super express goods', and included in the public timetables), were running between seven pairs of points.

With the development of fast freight services, containers were introduced. The first container service was operated by the Western Railway in 1966 between Bombay and Ahmedabad, using the fast freight service between those points. In 1967 came the Bombay–Delhi container service, and in the late 1960s other routes were covered (Howrah–Delhi, Madras–Bangalore, Bombay–Bangalore, Bombay–Madras, Bombay–Secunderabad). The five-ton container which was standardised for this traffic was designed to be suitable for use on both bg and mg, although of the initial services only Bombay–Bangalore involved break of gauge.

To make better use of containers, freight forwarders were accepted from 1968. These private businesses (equivalent to pool car operators in the USA and groupage contractors in

Britain) consolidated small shipments into container-size loads, thus qualifying for lower rates. Apparently the railways have found them very useful, for certain non-container traffic flows were soon opened to them. In the early 1970s container shipments were increasing fast (25,585 containers were booked in 1970–71) and could have increased even faster had more containers been available.

PASSENGER SERVICES

Indian railways carried 1284m passengers in 1950–51, and 2431m in 1970–71. Apart from the sheer growth of passenger services since independence, there have also been important qualitative changes, which tend to benefit the third-class passenger. One big change concerns passenger classes. Formerly there were, in theory, four classes: first, second, inter and third. In practice there were more, because the lower class passengers travelling by mail or express trains paid at a higher rate per mile. The abolition of first class seems to have been first mooted in 1945. First class traffic did not pay its way. Because of the ample space allowed each passenger, fewer passengers could be carried per train. After several schemes had been suggested and rejected, a substantial change was finally made in 1955. The old second class became first class, inter became second, and third class remained third class. It was intended that second class should also be abolished, and by the early 1970s this class had been removed from a number of trains, especially on branch line services.

As in post-revolutionary Russia, however, reduction of classes in principle was followed by proliferation in practice. One inevitable factor was the growth of air-conditioned travel. Air-conditioned coaches existed in very small numbers before World War II. After 1947 their importance increased for they replaced the old first class as the choice of the well-to-do traveller. In fact they were far more comfortable than the old first class, because they almost completely eliminated those bugbears of Indian railway travel, the pervasive and thick layering of dust, and high temperatures. To offer the less wealthy traveller the comforts of air-conditioned travel, air-conditioned chair cars were soon introduced. They did not include sleeping berths but the seats were much more comfortable than the wooden benches of normal third class coaches, while the number of passengers per coach was still quite high. Thus in the early 1970s there were really seven passenger classes: air-conditioned (in which it cost 51.45 rupees to travel 200 km), first class (25.75 rupees), air-conditioned chair (18.40 rupees), second class in mail or express trains (15.50 rupees), second class by ordinary (i.e. slow) train (12.60), third class mail and express (7.10 rupees) and third class ordinary (5.50 rupees). The fares quoted are for 1972. Rates per km were less for longer distances, the third class ordinary fare for 2,000 km being, for example, 40.90 rupees). It might be argued that the effective number of classes was nine because, for a surcharge, second and third class travellers in fast trains could be allocated sleeping space (in the superior classes berths were included in the price of the ticket; the typical first class compartment seated six persons by day and slept four by night; short-distance daytime passengers do not need reservations.)

Measures taken for the benefit of third-class passengers included an effort to improve the cleanliness of their accommodation, provision on certain fast trains of sleeping accommodation for them, fitting by 1959 of fans in all third class coaches, development of a reservation system, and opening of refreshment cars to all passengers in a train irrespective of class. To help the bewildered and probably illiterate traveller, passenger guides were appointed at main stations.

Perhaps the most important (at least from the public relations point of view) was the introduction on main routes of a new type of train, the *janata* ('people's') express for third-class passengers. These measures greatly benefitted poorer travellers, even though their effect was sometimes over-propagandised.

The original concept of the *janata* express was a vestibuled third-class-only train, running to mail train timings on a weekly basis. The popularity of these services has led to not only their introduction on additional routes, but to increased frequency (and the provision of non-vestibuled stock). Despite claims to the contrary, these trains did not run to the fastest schedules, nor were they unprecedented in British India. Up to about 1900, it is true, third class passengers had to travel by ordinary trains, which were extremely slow. Gradually however the railway companies began to provide fast services for third-class travellers, although fewer than demand warranted. In 1897 the EIR on the insistence of its Chairman, opened mail trains to third class passengers (previously EIR mail trains east of Allahabad carried only the upper classes and their servants). Then, in 1905, the EIR introduced its Howrah–Delhi Third-Class Express, which carried 570 third and 60 inter class passengers and no first or second. This train covered the 903 miles in 33hr 47min, (intermediate halts accounting for 7hr). The timing compares quite favourably with that of the present-day Howrah–Delhi Janata which, in 1972, was making the trip in 35hr 30min.

The prestigious air-conditioned Rajdhani Express needed in 1972, only 17hr 10min for the Howrah–Delhi run. This train was the first of a new series planned for the 1970s, of trains which would be comparable with European trains in speed and comfort. With diesel traction only one intermediate stop was necessary, at Kanpur. The maximum bg speed limit was raised for this service to 75mph and with the proposed introduction of a new bogie design it is hoped to raise this later to 100 mph. The Rajdhani Express includes air-conditioned sleeping cars and air-conditioned chair cars only. The latter are airline-style, with reclining seats and folding tables for attendant-served meals. A public address system enables passengers to be welcomed aboard by the strains of the 'Blue Danube', and to listen en route to All-India Radio news. Despite certain unforeseen snags such as the tendency of the less sophisticated chair car passengers to sleep on the floor and the lavatory queue in the morning, this pair of trains represented a notable step forward for the Indian passenger. In 1972 a second Rajdhani service was introduced, between Bombay and New Delhi. This, running over the Western Railway route, took 19hr 5min for the 861 miles, making no passenger stops en route. It compares with the 23hr 35min of the Frontier Mail, the 31hr 5min of the Janata, and over the 955-mile former GIP route, the 29hr of the Central Railway's Punjab Mail.

Other notable bg schedules in 1972 were those of the Howrah–Bombay mail via Nagpur, taking 36hr 40min for the 1220 miles (the corresponding mail via Allahabad took 47hr 50 min for 1350 miles). The celebrated Deccan Queen from Bombay to Poona took 3hr 25min for the 119 miles. The Howrah–Madras mail took 34hr 30min for 1030 miles. On the mg, the Ahmedabad–Delhi mail was timed at 23hr 55min for 579 miles. A number of new day trains were introduced with much publicity. Notable among these was the Taj Express. This was introduced in 1964 to serve tourists; leaving New Delhi early in the morning passengers could sightsee in Agra and then return by the same train to Delhi in the evening. It included three classes. In the single air-conditioned coach 27 large reclining armchairs were provided; in each of the two first class cars the 40 chairs also reclined, but were more modest; five third class cars with wooden seats provided another 360 places, and the formation was completed with a 30-seater restaurant car and a baggage car. In 1972, still with steam haulage, this train covered the 121 miles in exactly 3hr including one 3min stop. An innovation was the issue of return reservation tickets, the passenger returning from Agra in the same seat as for the outward trip.

A later addition to India's prestige trains was the Southern Railway's Brindavan Express, which provided a 5hr daytime service between Madras and Bangalore, stopping only thrice during the 220 mile journey. Like the Taj Express, this train was composed of special stock painted in a non-standard livery.

The blue-painted and vestibuled Deccan Queen, the blue-and-cream vestibuled Taj Express, and a few similar prestige trains, were not, however, typical. Most traffic is carried in traditional trains, consisting of maroon standard non-vestibuled stock offering first, second and third class accommodation.

Mention of just a few of the more notable trains is misleading as it obscures the general nature of the passenger services offered. In particular, the high density of passenger operations should be noted, and also the great variety of services operated over a given route. Operation of a large number of similar trains between two points, with passengers beyond those points preceding by connecting trains, was not the practice.

It was usual to provide from a given city as many different trains as possible, over the maximum number of different routes, running through to as many destinations as possible and (failing that) including through coaches to a large number of different destinations.

A big passenger station like Ahmedabad deals each day with more than 50 pairs of trains, and few of these pairs are alike in their destinations and services offered.

To take another random example, 1972 main-line passenger departures on the Western Railway from Bombay Central could be divided as follows (except where specified, these trains provided first, second, and third class accommodation): an evening and morning fast train to Ahmedabad; a slow train to Ahmedabad; a janata (third only) to Ahmedabad; three other trains to Ahmedabad and thence to Viramgam; namely an express (first and third), a janata (third) and a slow; the latter stopped at almost every station and took 23hr 36min for the 346 miles. To Delhi there was the bi-weekly Rajdhani Express (air-conditioned, and air-conditioned chair classes), a janata (third), a bi-weekly air-conditioned express including air-conditioned chair class, and first and third (on three additional days this train went beyond Delhi to Amritsar). There was also a weekly air-conditioned express to Delhi which on an additional day went through to Amritsar. In addition there was the daily Dehra Dun Express, and the daily Frontier Mail to Amritsar called at Delhi. To destinations closer to Bombay went the Flying Ranee (first and third to Surat), the Valsad Express (first and third) and the slow Baroda Passenger. Three of these trains (the Frontier Mail, the Rajdhani Express, and the air-conditioned expresses) were regularly diesel-hauled.

In 1972 very few passenger trains in India were diesel-hauled. Diesel locomotives produced a far better return on investment when hauling freight trains. Where diesels were used they did not, except for the Rajdhani Express, result in much faster schedules. Train formations were strengthened instead. Thus when in 1972 the mg Ahmedabad–Delhi Mail was dieselised, it ran to the same schedule but its load was increased from 15 to 18 vehicles.

The overwhelming problem of passenger services was not speed, but overcrowding. The impossibility of getting reservations at short notice without recourse to the black market and the tight packing of passengers in non-reserved services were a result of demand rising faster than services increased. Insufficient rolling stock and line capacity were the main hindrance to expansion, but in some places terminal facilities also were a limiting factor. By 1972, five Central Railway main-line trains from Bombay were terminated and originated at a suburban station, Dadar instead of Bombay Victoria. Faster average speeds through reducing the number of intermediate stops might have released some rolling stock through better utilisation, but local politicians not only objected to this but were sometimes prepared to mobilise their supporters against the railways.

FASTEST SCHEDULES ON SELECTED ROUTES, 1914 AND 1972

	1914 hr.	1972 hr.	1972 distance (miles)
Madras–Howrah	$39\frac{1}{2}$	34	1030
Madras–Bangalore	$10\frac{1}{2}$	5	220
Madras–Bombay	32	$32\frac{1}{4}$	783
Bombay–Howrah via Nagpur	$42\frac{1}{2}$	36	1222
Bombay–Howrah via Allahabad	37	$39\frac{3}{4}$	1352
Bombay–Delhi via GIP/CR	$29\frac{1}{2}$	29	958
Delhi–Lucknow	$8\frac{1}{4}$	$10\frac{1}{2}$	315
Kanpur–Lucknow	$1\frac{1}{4}$	2	45
Tuticorin–Madras (mg)	22	$18\frac{1}{4}$	304

Punctuality was poor in the late 1960s, but not so poor as some critics maintained. In 1971 the Minister of Railways proposed that staff responsible for late running should be punished (except on the Eastern Railway, where the social situation presumably made any improvement hopeless). In that year about 75 per cent of bg fast trains, and 80 per cent of mg arrived on time.

Railway staff were not always as courteous to passengers as they should have been, and this was made worse by the awe-inspiring clumsiness of the reservation system. All too often a third-class traveller would queue all night only to be told to join another queue. At many stations pretty displays of red, orange and green discs or coloured lights were installed so that would-be travellers would know which trains were fully booked for the next two or three weeks, which had a waiting list and which had still some accommodation. They could then make their written application for a train which they knew to be available. Too frequently, these coloured diagrams seemed to indicate only the situation the day before yesterday, because the staff did not keep them up to date.

Although the reservation system was cumbersome and did not seem entirely able to eliminate double-booking, the main fault in its operation was inept management and apathetic staff. At many stations where physical conditions were not especially good and train accommodation not especially plenti-ful but where the management and staff did make an effort, service was noticeably better. A radical improvement however seemed unlikely until computerisation could be introduced.

In 1970–71 about 10 per cent of passenger train-miles represented commuters travelling in electric multiple units (emus). In terms of numbers of passengers this proportion would naturally be higher. Four cities accounted for almost all commuter traffic: Bombay, where all commuters travelled in emu trains on the Western and Central Railways; Calcutta, where services were worked by emus and steam traction; Secunderabad (entirely steam); and Madras (steam on the bg from Madras Central, and mg emus from Madras Beach and Egmore).

Of all passenger traffic, commuter was the most unprofitable. The price of a monthly season ticket was equal to about nine or ten single journeys at ordinary fares, and fare levels were even more politically sensitive than other railway tariffs. The result was that other railway users were subsidising passengers who travelled by rail to work in India's most overcrowed cities —a situation not unknown in Britain and North America.

The lot of these passengers was not a happy one. At any time of day they could not be sure of a seat; at peak periods (totalling 6 hr daily) they could not be sure of even boarding the trains, except at originating stations. At intermediate stations train after train might halt, without offering a foothold either inside or outside. Passengers were so tightly packed that even pick-pocketing was impracticable. In effect, for the old and the weak, there was no train service. Relief of this situation was slow, due to shortage of capacity. In 1972 the train service seemed almost as dense as it could be. On the WR line out of Bombay, for example, starting at 04.28 and finishing at 01.00, 150 trains left for the suburbs (and on Sundays, only five fewer). The CR and WR Bombay commuter services taken together moved over 2m passengers daily. The population of metropolitan Bombay was approaching 4m, and 7m seems likely to be reached in the 1980s.

The construction of underground railways was one remedy, and in the early 1970s Russian engineers were helping to plan an underground for Calcutta. In Bombay, until such time as resources become available for an underground system, a number of palliatives are available. All these require investment however; and investment in services making such heavy losses is unlikely to be accorded high priority. Among these measures are quadrupling of tracks and the lengthening of trains. The standard train formation of nine cars is reckoned to accommodate 1800 first and third class passengers (sitting and standing, with the standing touching but not crushing each other). In fact, such trains in the rush hours often convey 3000 or more travellers. It has been suggested that the introduction of twelve-car trains would relieve this situation for a few years. Property owners would be among those pleased by this improvement, because the virtual impossibility of travelling to and from certain suburbs in the peak periods is bringing down property values.

CORRUPTION

From the earliest days of railways in India, corruption flourished. In 1937 the Wedgwood Committee commented that dishonesty was a vice as endemic in the railway service as in other Indian public services. World War II shortages and priority systems made things worse. After 1947, with ever more vigorous controls over economic life, corruption may also have increased, though conclusive statistics by the nature of things are not available. In 1953 a 12-man committee was appointed to study corruption on the railways, and its 200-page report is probably the most complete summary of the different opportunities open to railway staff ever made available in the history of the world's railways. As such, it deserves summary. Although India, with its tradition of family rather than state loyalties, faces special problems in this field, it is by no means alone; many of the examples to be quoted have their parallels in other countries.

According to the committee on corruption, consignors and consignees who did not pay railway officials the customary bribes might find various unpleasant things happening to their businesses. Scarce freight wagons would not be available for loading. Higher rates would be quoted for consignments. If they were sending food, covered wagons smelling of tar or kerosene would be offered to them. Wagons, especially if conveying perishables or livestock, would be held up on pretext of mechanical trouble. Staff would claim that consignments did not correspond to description on the invoices, and refuse to hand them over to the consignees.

A generous briber found all possible facilities granted to him. His goods would be registered (and paid for) at weights and values lower than they really were. Under a false name he could receive for loading empty wagons in excess of his allotment. Over short distances, with the connivance of guards, his consignments would be sent without charge and without invoice. If he was late delivering contracted goods, the railway clerks would offer him an ante-dated receipt. If he was late delivering his goods to the station the staff would obligingly declare that the wagons were unfit for immediate use, and he would thereby avoid financial penalty. If he consigned by the wagonload, he was allowed to overload his wagons. The wagons might be labelled to indicate more packages than were actually loaded, so that the consignor could make false loss claims. If a merchant was unable to unload wagons promptly, and thus liable to pay demurrage railway staff would delay the delivery of his wagons to the unloading point. If he consigned perishables, and the market was falling, his shipments might be delayed so that he could make claims for deterioration. His consignments might be addressed to Government departments so as to obtain priority, and then switched to their real destination somewhere en route. His parcels might be booked as the baggage of passengers who had no connection with his business. This pattern of bribery was especially advantageous for the clerical staff, but to ensure co-operation from other grades a proportion of their illicit earnings was distributed to stationmasters, superintendents, and participating workers.

Bernard de Villeroi, in his *History of the North Western Railway*, had this to say in 1896:

> . . . When tickets were being issued a policeman stood at the ticket window to keep order, with one arm stretched across the passage. No one, no matter how poor, could get along unless he paid one pice, this was for the police. The booking clerk when giving change would give something too little and when the recipient complained, the policeman removed his arm and let in a rush of impatient passengers, who soon pushed the man away from the window . . .

According to the evidence of the committee investigating corruption, things had not changed very much in the present century. Among the corrupt practices which passengers endured were the following. Booking office windows would open late, causing congestion. Because so many passengers could not read their tickets, short-changing and the issue of tickets to destinations short of those asked for and paid for was easy. Shortage of accomodation, as with freight traffic, offered golden opportunities. Reservations and tickets would be sold, for a commission, to black marketeers who would resell them at inflated prices on street corners or to travel agents. Baggage porters would occupy unreserved seats in the carriage sidings, holding them for passengers waiting at the station who would pay good prices for the service. Generous passengers would be allowed to carry into their compartments all kinds of freight masquerading as hand baggage. Berths reserved for VIPs, railway officials, passengers joining en route, and due to be released for waiting-list passengers, could be obtained by people willing to pay a heavy fee. As regards ticketless travel, this problem is dealt with separately, but in view of the subsequent scale of this problem it is interesting to note that the corruption committee reported that most passengers who travelled without tickets did so with the collusion of the railway staff.

Corrupt practices also appeared in recruiting and promotions of staff. The local executive officers who engaged Class IV staff often charged a fixed fee for appointing an applicant. Although it was Railway Service Commissions which recruited Class III staff, the members of commissions were often in profitable touch with outside brokers who offered railway jobs in exchange for a fee. In railway training institutions it was not uncommon for directors to charge a fee for passing students through the examinations. Medical departments charged fees for issuing true or false sickness certificates. Doctors might recommend spectacles from opticians who paid them commissions. Expensive or scarce medicines were reserved for high officials or the black market.

As in the nineteenth century, there were always railwaymen who would use their special advantages to pursue criminal activities. The high loss claims paid out by Indian railways were largely due to thefts by railwaymen. Break-of-gauge transhipment stations were good hunting grounds for these thieves. For those without access to such points were other possi-

Page 123 (above) One of the GIPR's original Metrovick electric locomotives, still in service for freight and banking; (below) CR Bombay–Thana suburban emu at Parel

Page 124 (above) Electric locomotives await the right-away from Moghal Sarai yard in 1972. The nearest unit is of Class WAM1, the other of Class WAG4; *(below)* Baroda (WR) in 1970. A Class H 4–6–0, the standard passenger engine of the former BBCIR, pulls in while a WP Pacific stands in the bay

bilities. A wagon containing valuable goods could be declared to be in bad order and then pilfered at a convenient time. Or it could be shunted into an isolated siding for the same purpose. Chalk marks on the sides of wagons with especially valuable contents would be a guide for lineside thieves. Train crews might stop trains at prearranged points to facilitate theft. If train crews were not co-operative, trains could still be halted in isolated spots by cutting the brake pipe, or by greasing the rails on gradients.

Pilferage of locomotive coal was a problem in itself. It was traditional, and accepted, that at points where engines cleaned their fires the poorer or juvenile members of the local communities could rake through the hot ashes, collecting incompletely burned pieces for resale. From this it was a short step to lineside scavengers themselves poking the grates of stationary locomotives, in quest of larger unburnt lumps. Sometimes, too, the fireman out of charity or because his relatives lived in the neighbouhood, would put a shovelful of coal over the side. These practices developed until some enginemen regularly deposited a few shovelfuls of coal at certain points, picking up in recompense bags of money hung on sticks at the trackside.

In locomotive depots, coal disappeared at a noticeable rate, often finding its way to coal merchants for resale. After 1947, sporadic coal economy drives were launched to save money, especially on the WR and SR, whose fuel had always been expensive, because of the distance from the coalfields. Quite creditable percentage economies were usually achieved, but it is hard to know whether such successes were a result of better firing or simply of a temporary tightening up of controls.

OTHER SOCIAL PROBLEMS

After World War II especially, the Indian railways were plagued with social problems which were not really of their own making and could be tackled only on a national scale. They took the form of theft, sabotage, disruption, mass ticketless travel and widespread pulling of passenger train alarm chains. There was one common factor in all these phenomena: the railways were an easy prey. As a State-owned public utility, they could serve as targets for those wishing to vent their spleen against the Government. As the largest nationalised industry, they could be robbed with a clear conscience by those who believed in private enterprise. As a large and impersonal institution, they could be defrauded without qualms by millions of ordinary people.

The Indian Railways annual report for 1961–62 mentioned 40,065 cases during the year of unauthorised pulling of train alarm chains. In 1970–71 there were nearly 362,000 such cases (nearly a thousand a day). Some of these alarm signals were given so as to stop the train within walking distance of a passenger's destination. Some were intended as practical jokes, and others simply to work off resentment against the railways or fellow passengers. (The author in 1963 watched the halting of a fast mail train by a passenger getting the worst of an argument over the rightful possession of a first class berth). In addition, a small proportion of the chain pullings were by, or in aid of, thieves who found this the best method of joining and escaping from trains. On a railway system as intensively worked as India's, chaos could be caused by each delay of this kind. As with most railway lawlessness, the problem of chain pulling was most acute on the ER, SER and NER.

Attempts to master it were hampered by lack of co-operation by the public, which seemed to side with the culprits. Only rarely would passengers identify a chain-puller for the benefit of the police. The incidence of chain pulling was slow to respond to counter measures, largely because effective measures could only be cumbersome in the absence of public co-operation. It was possible, for example, to make a few arrests by detailing plain clothes policemen in trains which were regularly subject to this trouble, This, however was expensive and not worth while in trains that were only intermittently affected. The most effective measure was the removal or blocking-off of alarm chains. This was done in some areas, and immediately produced complaints of more frequent attacks on passengers at night, and on women passengers. Discontent in turn led to the restoration of communication cords in ladies-only compartments, and to their unblocking at night. The remedy had become almost as costly as the disease. Some railways tried to educate the public by arranging lectures and film shows to discourage this and other anti-social conduct. Such efforts to produce a more socially-conscious public, which would oppose the delaying of 1000 passengers by a single chain-puller, seemed to offer the best prospects in the long term.

The ticketless traveller was well-known in India before independence, but somehow, when Indian railways were considered to be a British affair, it was not widely regarded as a misdemeanour. This legacy probably made ticketless travel such a problem after 1947. As with alarm chain pulling, the situation was aggravated by public sympathy for defaulters. In the early 1970s it was believed that about one-tenth of actual passenger-miles were not paid for. This represented an amount which could have meant the difference between profit and loss for the railways.

Travelling in accommodation of a higher class than that paid for was a minor problem in comparison. Temptations leading to ticketless travel were many. Overcrowding meant that passengers were resentful, and failure to buy a ticket could become an act of revenge. The crowds at booking office windows and lethargic ticket clerks often made purchase of tickets really difficult. Overcrowding and the absence of vestibule gangway connections between vehicles made ticket inspection difficult. Nor were some inspectors unresponsive to bribes or threats. The railway police were often handicapped by the apathy of their opposite numbers in the local police.

Many passengers, despite an increase of penalties sanctioned in 1969, regarded ticketless travel as an exciting gamble. Thus in 1972 on the NR a wedding party of 23 third-class travellers were found to be without tickets in the Amritsar–Delhi Janata Express. Fined by a railway magistrate on the spot, they cheerfully paid up and continued their journey.

From time to time drives and campaigns were launched to worst the ticketless traveller. Impressive (and accurate) statistics were produced to show that ticket sales suddenly increased by 10 per cent or more as passengers decided that discretion was called for, and to show how the number of arrests of ticketless travellers had nevertheless increased. Within a few months however, of the termination of a drive, it usually seemed that things were just as bad as before. In 1948, for example, on the Eastern Punjab Railway, officials, police, and a special railway magistrate descended on an unsuspecting train at a secluded spot, halting it by means of detonators. After the terrified passengers had realised that this was not, after all, an attack by bandits, they discovered that they were surrounded by a police cordon and were invited to produce their tickets. Of the 1000 or so travellers, about 100 were ticketless, and were fined by a lineside magistrate's court. Since fines were low (and even after 1969 were still low enough to make ticketless travel a worthwhile gamble) this step had no long-term effect.

It is possible, however, that new moves made in 1971 may have marked a turning of the tide. The State of Haryana, an area of the Punjab where ticketless travel had always been endemic, was selected. Raids of a conventional type by police and railway magistrates were undertaken. What was new was the co-operation of the local government. Local police and railway police could work together and make advance plans thanks to co-operation already achieved by the Railway Minister and the Prime Minister of Haryana. Similar co-operation with other States was envisaged. Elimination of the ticketless passenger, it was believed, would not only increase revenue but also go some way toward reducing alarm chain pulling, because the latter was a device often resorted to by ticketless travellers seeking to evade inspectors.

Pilferage of railway property, as well as of railway freight, remained a problem, especially in the troubled North Eastern States. In 1972 the Railway Minister, taking a more serious view of this than many railway officials, indicated that about one seventh of Indian Railways' coal purchases was lost through pilferage.

Thefts of other railway property were about equal in value to the coal loss. 'Pilferage', like many of the terms used to describe the railways' troubles, was not perhaps the right word to describe a massive well-planned assault on railway property with the surreptitious backing of respected figures.

The ER and SER suffered especially from large-scale crime in the late 1960s and early 1970s. These two railways together accounted for about 60 per cent of Indian Railways' freight traffic, and used about 40 per cent of the bg wagon stock. Disruption of these two railways could, and did, have serious repercussions on the other systems. Scarce metals, especially copper, were a prime target. On the ER in 1970 an average of about 100 freight and passenger vehicles were damaged by theft daily and the ER could restore them only at the rate of 50 a day. Brake blocks, brass bearings, pipes, dynamos, and fans were the trophies most favoured by thieves. Whenever a train was halted it was in danger. Sometimes, the train might restart unexpectedly, in which case the thief might suffer serious injury, but this was a game which was worth the candle.

Even more worthwhile, though demanding some finesse, was the removal of copper catenary wire on electrified lines. On the ER about 17,000m of copper wire were stolen in 1968, and this increased to 35,000m in 1970. Such abstraction of live wire could be very lucrative, thanks to the black market demand for copper.

Signalling and telecommunication installations were even better targets, for they provided copper at ground level with less risk of electrocution. Transformers also had a very high resale value. On the ER alone in 1970 there were over 10,000 cases of wire thefts from signalling and telecommunication installations. The effect of such thefts was disruption of train services to an extent easy to imagine. On the SER in the 1970–71 working year, there were 186 cases of catenary theft, resulting in 1078hr of suspended electric services. Because of attacks on signalling and telecommunications, breakdowns of train control in individual sections occurred over 5000 times on the SER, totalling over 51,000hr. It seemed that the more a railway was modernised, the more vulnerable it became. Concurrently the SER suffered from over 40,000 cases of alarm chain pulling and, as if even this was not enough, endured 32 civil disturbances which interfered with train services. In early 1971 the ER and SER, which to satisfy the country's needs should have originated at least 6500 loaded coal wagons, were only loading a daily average of 5500.

Disturbances in West Bengal, in which both the ER and SER had many lines, were rife at that time. This is why these two railways were so badly affected by social turmoil at a time when other railways worked almost normally, apart from suffering side effects of the ER's disabilities. For example, non-delivery of coal from the East sometimes meant train cancellations on other railways.

What happened in the late 1960s and early 1970s makes an interesting, perhaps unique, case study of railway operation in circumstances of social near-disintegration. Possibly the near-collapse (or survival) of the railways in the eastern areas is only a foretaste of what could happen in other parts of the world in response to political, economic and social breakdown in conditions of over-population.

For example, in October 1969 a student was detected travelling without a ticket at Sealdah terminus in Calcutta. After a violent argument more than 100 students from various colleges attacked the railway offices, beat up railwaymen and damaged whatever was damageable in the station. With sympathetic members of the general public, they then held up railway services for 12hr. In June of the same year about 200 armed men held up a local train near Calcutta in order to seek out the somewhat disliked rice-smugglers. The following month there was a case of a squatting, when a section of railway was brought to a standstill by demonstrators who sat on the track as a protest against the police.

Squatting became widespread. It was in direct line of descent from the non-violent resistance practised by Gandhi, and accordingly had wide popular appeal even though its objectives might not have been approved by Gandhians. There were two kinds of squat, those directed against the railway and those in protest at some action quite unconnected with the railways but for which the railways were a suitable target. Not only did the railways represent 'them', but by their nature they provided spectacular and fairly easily achieved results. Squats directed against the railways might be relatively spontaneous protest against uncomfortable or unpunctual trains, or they might be planned manifestations aimed at securing concessions for local interests. In the latter variety it was not unknown for local politicians to take part. In 1972, for example, a former Bihar minister and prominent local Congress Party member encouraged people at Dhanbad on the ER to sit on the tracks in order to persuade the Railway Ministry to introduce a Dhanbad–Patna passenger train (and a few months later, perhaps by coincidence and perhaps not, such a train was introduced).

An occurrence in 1970 illustrated how fairly minor incidents could start a chain reaction. In August a local train to Calcutta Howrah was the scene of what was euphemistically described as 'a lively altercation' between some assertive passengers and a band of alleged rice smugglers. When the smugglers detrained at a suburban station somebody, as a contribution to the argument, disconnected the brake pipe. Passengers, disgruntled by the resultant delay, then descended on the guard and motorman and beat them up. As a result of all this the train reached Howrah 12min late. Passengers thereupon beat up the same motorman and a relief guard. The motorman was taken to hospital and the railwaymen at Howrah refused to carry on. Railway officers addressed the railway staff and persuaded them to resume work, but on leaving this meeting an angry crowd of delayed passengers began to threaten them. One irate passenger was arrested at this point, and this appears to have been the first and only arrest of the day. Eventually the trains started moving again after a 7hr stoppage. Intimidation of train crews and train burning was quite common in the Calcutta area. A train which was delayed, say, by theft of catenary, could easily become the scene of violence. At one stage the train crews of Calcutta threatened to strike until they were properly protected. On the other side of the country, the Bombay suburban services were similarly attacked, but on a much smaller scale.

With theft, beatings-up, bomb-throwing and other disorders continually occurring, and very little action taken against the perpetrators (who, it was alleged, were often protected from the law by the influence of local politicians) it is not surprising that train sabotage began to increase. Removal of a rail was the favourite method, usually on a fast running section. Casualties tended to be high.

Railway police work was shared, not always happily, by two organisations, the GRP and the RPF. Each State Government had its police force, part of which was in the form of the Government Railway Police. The GRP was largely financed from railway budgets, but the railways had no control, and not much influence, over it. They did, however, possess their own Railway Protection Force. The RPF was set up in 1957 to replace the Watch & Ward organisations which the various railways had established after World War I to combat a wave of theft. It was answerable ultimately to Delhi, but each railway operated its own RPF establishment. By 1963 the RPF totalled about 53,000 men, all literate. It also included some tracker dogs, the most perspicacious of which were accommodated in ultra-modern kennels equipped with electric fans.

The purpose of the RPF was to reduce pilferage and its main function was the organisation of patrols in yards and depots where thieves could be expected. It had rather limited powers of search and arrest, and did not conduct criminal investigations or prosecutions. Nor was it responsible for the maintenance of law and order. All these functions belonged to the GRP, which in theory would act on information passed on to it by the RPF. In practice, this did not always happen. The RPF was a railway affair but the GRP was answerable to the local

Page 133 (above) Sack-and-a-half of locomotive fuel en route to an unknown destination (1972); (below) Ahmedabad station concourse in an off-peak period

Page 134 (above) Locomotive driver and fireman of an SR XD class locomotive; (centre) RPF guard on duty at Ahmedabad (WR); (below) Head-coaling on the NER

Page 135 (above) Swiss-built (SLM) rack locomotive propelling the SR metre gauge Nilgiri Express to Ootacamund, has its fire cleaned at an intermediate station; (below) narrow gauge at Dabhoi in 1970. Two standard ZB engines enter the station to pick up their trains, while an older 4–6–0 awaits departure

Page 136 (above) Near Baroda, on the narrow gauge line of the former Cutch State railway, a mixed train passes beneath the WR main line; (below) Saoner Junction on the SER narrow gauge near Nagpur. A ZE 2–8–2 waits with a branch train as a ZDM diesel brings in a main-line train to Nagpur

State Government not necessarily composed of energetic or public-spirited men.

Some criminals, it seems certain, were protected persons. Secondly, even with the best will in the world the GRP was less fitted than the RPF to conduct railway investigations. A competent investigator needed railway knowledge and experience, and must know railway procedures so as to detect suspicious variations. The RPF did valuable service with its armed guards and patrols, but it might have done more if given more scope. Some of its members themselves succumbed to temptation and participated in theft on their own account or in co-operation with outsiders. Others were killed in the course of their duties. Inside the RPF there was a small Special Intelligence Branch. This, by choice, was an obscure body which seemed to possess some of the characteristics of conventional secret police forces. It dealt with 'political' matters and used informers to gain advance information of such phenomena as squatting, sabotage, and perhaps strikes. The author recalls visiting one of its officers' homes, and being served tea and cakes on crockery purloined from a station restaurant.

'Borrowing' of railway crockery and cutlery by policemen is not perhaps a serious matter. What the outside observer found somewhat puzzling was a failure on the part of responsible officials to face the real underlying problems. Track patrols were intensified. Steel-reinforced aluminium wire began to be used in place of copper. Thieves were more often apprehended. Nevetherless it was the small men who went to jail. The organizers and the purchasers of stolen materials seemed to continue unscathed. Railwaymen found to be dishonest were punished, usually by dismissal.

Discussion of the problem seemed to involve much tut-tutting, with little searching analysis. At a time when one ton in every seven of locomotive coal was being stolen, this author was assured both by railway and RPF officials that coal pilferage was only a marginal and petty problem. While enduring a ride in a first-class six-seater compartment from

Patna to Benares, containing four ticket-holding passengers and 12 ticketless students, the author was assured (after the departure of the unwelcome guests) that they were 'rowdies'. The passenger who made this comment, it later transpired, was a senior police officer going to a conference. He later described how he had used one of his official rubber stamps to enable him to acquire a duty-free camera. When trains were burned in Calcutta or Bombay the favourite word was 'vandalism'. But calling train wreckers vandals explains nothing; analysis was needed, not name-calling.

Was there any significance in the fact that it was the ER, SER, NR, and NER which suffered most, and the SR and WR least, from chain-pulling? The first four railways served the traditional areas of orthodox Hinduism whereas the latter served populations which liked to regard themselves as more sophisticated and progressive. The first four also, served areas which were traditionally the most poor and overpopulated of India. Could any analogy be drawn between overcrowded Calcutta commuters beating up railwaymen and that memorable occasion when overcrowded London commuters refused to leave a broken-down train when requested to do so? What was the influence of history? The first case of railway sabotage, after all, appears to have been an attempt in 1907 to blow up the Lieutenant Governor's train in Bengal.

In 1942, coinciding with the threat of Japanese invasion, there was a wave of sabotage on Indian railways, especially in Bihar. Rails were removed, irreplaceable signalling apparatus smashed and copper wire stolen. In those days the saboteurs could esteem themselves heroes, but three decades later yesterday's freedom-fighting had become today's vandalism. Track squatting was similarly an activity which in the days of the British *raj* was highly regarded by many of those who subsequently held high positions in independent India.

ACCIDENTS

Accident statistics were compiled by the Government from the early days of railways, but their interpretation is not easy.

The year 1869–70 was considered a bad year, with 31 fatalities among passengers (1.87 per million), this total not including those who were victims of their own negligence, trespassers, and railwaymen. In addition, 132 passengers died of natural causes, such as heatstroke or cholera. Accidents in the early years were uncomplicated, being mainly collisions, derailments and, in the rainy season, failures of bridges.

Animals were sometimes responsible. A bad accident on the BBCIR was caused by an errant buffalo, too small to be caught up by the cowcatcher. The BBCI was blamed at the inquiry for its lack of fencing, and responded with the classic retort that a lineside fence would keep animals in as well as out. On the EIR in 1869 the locomotive of a night freight train puffing noisily and glowing red, threw an encampment of 70 elephants into a panic. One bull elephant met the locomotive head-on, killing himself and the driver, and derailing the train. In a later period, a derailment was caused on the NWR by a rat which had climbed into the brake pipe of coaches standing on a siding. When these were connected to a locomotive, the rat was suffocated, sucked along the pipe, and brought to rest at a constriction, effectively blocking the system. When the driver applied the brake for a speed restriction, there was no response. The Ghat sections of the GIP witnessed several night accidents; for a time in 1870 all services over the Thull Ghat were daylight only. The Lonavla accident of 1867 was remarkable in that a rescue party was despatched even before the accident occurred; a crewless shunting engine ran away from the Lonavla yard and a collision with a Poona–Bombay passenger train was seen to be inevitable. The Lonavla station master sent a rescue engine to pick up the casualties. As had been forecast in the 1840s, bg trains were less likely to be blown over than mg. Up to 1891 five bg trains had been victims of high winds, whereas on the still young mg lines ten trains had already been blown over.

The widow of one of the passengers killed at Lonavla was later awarded what were considered to be princely damages (nearly £10,000) at Lewes Assizes in England. According to some accounts, while European victims of Indian railway accidents could hope to receive just compensation, native passengers were less fortuate. Railway officers, it was alleged, did all they could to minimise the injuries received by passengers, so that any compensation would at least be small.

The management of the State-operated EIR won much disapprobation after the Bihta accident of 1937, in which over 100 pasengers were killed when the Punjab–Howrah Mail was derailed. An XB Pacific, restricted to 45mph in the monsoon season, hauled the train because the usual 4–6–0 was not available and even though the schedule could not be kept without exceeding 45mph. The EIR refused to accept the uncomplimentary report of the Government Inspector, but the subsequent judicial inquiry concurred that the railway had been negligent. The case was not finally settled until 1942. Meanwhile the EIR was accused of tampering with witnesses and seeking to evade responsibility. The misgivings aroused led to the decision in 1940 that the Senior Government Inspector of Railways should be independent of the Railway Board.

The statistics reveal few clear trends for the first half of this century. State-managed railways had a worse record than company-managed lines, but the figures were not really conclusive. As might be expected, there was a marked increase of accidents in 1947–50. The peak was in 1948–49, with 2781 serious accidents reported. Over succeeding years the accident rates noticeably decreased, although the general public, interested less in accident rates than in the number of spectacular accidents, believed that the rate was rising. Public disquiet reached a preliminary peak in the mid-1950s, when there were several accidents with high casualty figures. After one such accident, that of the mg Madras–Tuticorin Express in 1956, which cost 154 lives, the Railway Minister resigned in a rare acknowledgement of ministerial responsibility.

Disquiet was renewed in the early 1960s and committees were appointed to study the problem. These reported later in the decade. They observed that despite increasing traffic the number of accidents was falling. In fact, even in the early

1960s, when it was alleged that Indian railways were unsafe, the rate of accidents per train-mile was lower than in Canada and the USA, although higher than in Western Europe. In 1962–63, there were 98 collisions and 1316 derailments. The following year was similar, but by 1970–71 the figures had been reduced to 59 collisions and 648 derailments. Train fires, which figured prominently in the accident statistics, were similarly reduced.

Measures to reduce the accident rate included the usual exhortations to staff, reinforced by films, posters, and pamphlets, and a limited number of signalling improvements. Special officers responsible for safety were appointed on all railways with the duty not only of advising, but also checking. All the railways organised week-long 'safety camps', in which operating staff with responsibility for train movements could discuss safety matters without the inhibitions they might feel when discussing such problems on their home ground. A 'psycho-technical cell' was formed to conduct surveys and research into the psychology of accidents. With well over half of all accident caused by human failure (and one third of deaths caused by drivers' lapses) it was essential to find means of detecting staff who were most accident-prone. To cope with an increased incidence of tampering with the track, rail welding was speeded up on the main lines, and the use of reversed jaw sleepers with conventional sleepers was recommended so as to make rail removal more difficult. Only a very small proportion of track sabotage was successful, partly because removing a rail is not as easy as it looks. In 1950–61, there were 990 train wrecking attempts, of which only 3 per cent were successful. But successful wrecking tended to cause heavy casualties.

NARROW-GAUGE AND HILL RAILWAYS

In 1971 the narrow-gauge (narrower than one metre) lines accounted for less than 8 per cent of the route mileage, and little more than 1 per cent of the passengers and tonnage carried by Indian Railways. Nevertheless, in their own localities they played an important role. Although most narrow gauge lines were short branches from a bg or mg main line, some were long (for example, the 204-mile main line of the former Barsi Light Railway) and some which formed networks covering wide areas. Of the latter, the lines radiating from Gwalior (the former 2ft gauge Scindia State Railway), the former Gaekwar of Baroda's State Railway's narrow-gauge lines radiating from Dabhoi, and the former BNR's narrow-gauge system in the Nagpur area were the most notable examples.

Whereas on the typical narrow-gauge lines picturesque inefficiency and local colour were always well in evidence, the large systems sometimes gave a more purposeful impression. Dabhoi, for example, dealt with 14 pairs of heavily loaded passenger trains daily and was not at all the sleepy kind of station associated with the narrow gauge. On the BNR (now SER) narrow-gauge system originally built as a 142 mile link between the BNR and GIP main lines but extended subsequently to a total of over 600 miles, German-built diesel locomotives shared the traffic with steam traction. Four-axle wagons were used, many of 23 tonnes. Like some other narrow-gauge lines, it operated a railway post office on its main passenger train, a 14-vehicle formation.

Most of the narrow-gauge lines faced severe road competition, but low fares protected their third-class traffic. In the long term their future would in most cases be a choice between conversion to bg, or closure. Closure, however, was not easy, because for local inhabitants the railway was the cheapest means of access to the neighbouring towns. By the early 1970s very few sections had been widened, although there were proposals to convert to bg the main narrow-gauge line of the former BNR system between Gondia and Jabalpur, and two of the Dabhoi lines of the WR. One line, the Kangra Valley Railway from Pathankot, was partially relaid to the same 2ft 6in gauge when its original roadbed was inundated by a hydro-electric project.

The Indian hill railways, like the narrow-gauge lines, have

perhaps attracted more attention than their importance warrants. Especially is this true of the Darjeeling–Himalaya Railway, now part of the Northeast Frontier Railway. This 2ft gauge line with its 1 in 20 grades, and its spectacular loops and reversals, has always been a favourite among railway enthusiasts and among those who appreciate striking engineering and scenery. It was built to provide access to the hill station of Darjeeling.

Other resorts favoured under British rule were Simla, in the Himalayas conveniently close to Delhi; Ootacamund in the Nilgiris; and Matheran, near Bombay. All these had their own access railways. The 60-mile Kalka–Simla line linked India's summer capital with the bg terminus of Kalka. Of 2ft 6in gauge, it climbed 5000ft and was worked by the NWR. After 1947 it became part of the NR and was soon dieselised.

The 2ft gauge Neral–Matheran line connects the GIP station at Neral with the hill resort, climbing nearly 2400ft in its 12 miles. Closed during the monsoon, in the hot season it operates a busy timetable, and in the early 1970s was using both steam and diesel traction. Technically the most interesting of the hill railways is the Nilgiri Railway, an isolated mg connection between the bg railhead at Mettupalaiyam and the hill resort at Ootacamund. There are 1 in 25 adhesion grades, and even steeper stretches where the Abt rack system is used. Trains recently were still hauled by tank locomotives built in Switzerland. Four pairs of trains are operated daily, although only two cover the entire 29 miles. Recalling past associations, the wayside stations still bear their old names: Lovedale, Hillgrove, and Runnymede. By the early 1970s the four hill railways showed no sign of imminent closure. They represent large financial losses for the zonal railways which operate them, but to many they seem indispensible, despite road competition.

CHAPTER 4

Infrastructure and Rolling Stock

BRIDGES

DESPITE spectacular passages of the Western Ghats by the two GIPR main lines from Bombay and some hill sections elsewhere, the greatest obstacle to Indian railway building has been not mountains, but rivers. By 1971 there were 104,368 bridges in service, of which 8424 were classified as major, and most were over water. In any given year several new bridges were under construction, and others (354 in 1971) are being rebuilt, regirdered or otherwise strengthened.

Techniques of bridge building have changed. The brick arches of the early structures were superseded by girders and later, as in the 1971 Farakka Bridge, by pre-stressed concrete. But the treacherous nature of Indian rivers has always been a problem. River beds which might be perfectly dry for eight months of the year become mile-wide fast-flowing rivers during the monsoon, and without warning rivers change their course. Hence the great length of so many bridges and their abutments.

The EIR's Sone Bridge, completed in 1863, had 28 decked spans of 157ft each (making, with abutments, 4,726ft) mounted on brick piers sunk to a depth of 32ft below low water. In those days little was known of the scouring effect of the fast currents, and there were many cases of piers being undermined. The Sutlej Bridge of the NWR lost some of its piers within six years of completion. This bridge, one of the first of the traditional long bridges, had 38 100ft single lattice wrought-iron truss girder spans, many of which were left high and dry when the Sutlej changed its course. The same railway's bridge over the Beas took a locomotive with it when it collapsed. The 1887 Dufferin Bridge over the Ganges at Benares had piers sunk to 120ft below low water. By that time scour was better understood and this bridge stood firm, being re-girdered (and renamed) in 1947. 1887 was also the year in which the Hooghly was bridged, 28 miles from Howrah. India's longest bridge over the Upper Sone, was built in 1900 and measures 10,052ft.

The girder bridge, often carrying both the railway and a road, was regarded as most suitable for Indian conditions. There was only one steel arch bridge, on the narrow-gauge Kangra Valley line. Methods of construction, however, have varied. The 2,460ft bridge over the Jumna at Delhi, opened in 1866, was fortified on the insistence of the Government. The railway approach to the bridge included a drawbridge, while the abutments had a loopholed wall, with strong gates across the road. The BBCIR standardisation of components under Kennedy was carried far, with a uniform 62ft 5in girder span, with each set of holes from the same template, each screw from the same thread, and all piers consisting of 2ft 6in cast-iron cylinders filled with concrete. This standard-isation was not only a logistic advantage, but also enabled constructors to work faster, after they had become familiar with the design. Thus the large bridge over the Tapti, consist-ing of 30 standard spans, was built in only eight working months. However, Kennedy's much vaunted route with its easy gradients and excellent bridges was subject to flooding until, in the early nineteen seventies, it was finally decided to avoid future washouts and flooding by raising the line on its most exposed sections.

It would be hard to find a greater contrast than that between the BBCIR flat water-level route to the North from Bombay and its rival the GIPR's two lines over the Western Ghats. The Thull Ghat incline on the GIPR route to the North is nine miles long, including four miles of 1 in 37, six viaducts, 15 bridges, 12 tunnels, and a reversing station.

The Bhore Ghat line to Poona and Madras is over 15 miles

long and includes a reversing station, 25 tunnels and eight viaducts. In places the ravines are so steep that one track is laid on a benched-out terrace and the other supported by arches or an embankment. The first engine to climb the incline in 1862 was greeted by a landslide which filled in a cutting, necessitating construction of another tunnel. Built entirely by contract, the Bhore Ghat section took over seven years to build, and at the peak employed 42,000 workers. In subsequent years sections of this line were rebuilt or realigned. As early as 1867 one of the viaducts was replaced. This viaduct, according to the local inhabitants, was dangerous, but the authorities said that the small cracks which had been noticed were longstanding and of no structural consequence. But the eight arch structure collapsed half-an-hour after a train had crossed it and just four days after it had been inspected and pronounced safe by the railway's engineers. A platelayer who was on the viaduct at the time felt the ground giving way under him and ran as fast as he could, with his eyes closed in terror, to the end of the viaduct. When he opened his eyes the structure had disappeared.

TRACK AND STATIONS

The GIP's first line had 65lb wrought-iron double-headed rails, laid longitudinally on stone sleepers. Soon both bullhead and flatbottom rails were in use in India. The Indian Midland Railway, built in 1890, used 80lb flatbottom rails. Bg light railways were not favoured, the narrower gauges being used where track was to be laid at pioneer standards. When the mg was adopted, 40lb rail was fixed as the standard, although 30lb was used on some lightly trafficked lines. With 40lb rail, axleloads of six tons were permissible, but some mg lines, because of their success, were soon upgraded. The mg Rajputana–Malwa Railway, for example, was relaid with 50lb rails. The most substantially built of the narrow gauge lines, the Barsi Light Railway, used 30lb rail.

By 1914 90lb flatbottom rail was regarded as the standard for bg trunk routes, permitting a 22.5 ton axleload and a maximum speed of 60mph. This rail was still widely used on main lines in the early 1970s but, as its life was only about 15 years on the busier sections, it is being superseded by a new 105lb fb type designed by the Railway Design & Standards Organisation, capable of taking 25-ton axleloads. On the mg in 1914, 60lb rails allowing 13-ton axleloads and 45mph speeds were in use on busy sections. Six decades later a 75lb rail (17.5-ton axleloads) was replacing the 60lb type. The mg, like the narrow gauges also re-used worn rails discarded by the bg. Rail joint welding, typically of three to five standard 42ft 8in rails, is widely practised, and a programme for long-welded rails was evolved in the late 1960s. Rail welding, apart from eliminating joints, also makes removal of rails harder for saboteurs.

Sleepers were mainly of timber in the early days, but cast-iron plate and steel trough designs later became widespread, although wood still predominated on the mg. Pot sleepers (resembling two inverted iron pots joined by a spacing bar) became popular because they were cheap, but they had poor lateral stability, were difficult to pack, tended to creep, and entailed wide spacing at the rail joint. Despite these defects they continued in use, but the later standard bg sleeper is of cast iron with its ends not flat but forming two pockets and a keel. In the 1970s a monobloc prestressed concrete bg sleeper has come into use, and also a two-block reinforced concrete design.

With annual floods, and wide daily temperature ranges which aggravate expansion and contraction problems, thorough track inspection has always been emphasised on Indian railways. The system of inspection established in British times survived after 1947. The Railway Inspectorate comprises the Chief Government Inspector of Railways, with the Government Inspectors who report to him. Each Government Inspector has a special train which conveys him, the General Manager of the railway concerned, and the District officers. All lines are inspected annually. Also enjoying an inspection coach and locomotive are the railway's District engineers, but the more humble District permanent way engineers, and the Sub-Divisional assistant engineers use the time-honoured inspection trolley. This consists of four wheels, a platform, and a forward facing seat whose legs fit into sockets on the platform. There is a hand or foot brake, and usually an umbrella. Two red flags are compulsorily flown. Propulsion is by four pushers. Two rest on the platform while two others, each running barefoot on the top surface of the rail, push. On down gradients or when momentum is gained, all the pushers rest. The trolley moves at about 10mph and can be dismantled and removed from the track in less than 20 seconds. Track maintenance is at fixed intervals, depending on the type of track and the traffic density. However, by the late 1960s a system of directed maintenance was being introduced with work carried on not according to a schedule, but according to needs as revealed by inspections. To reduce line occupation by engineers on busy sections, tamping machines were introduced in the 1960s to replace the traditional hand packing. Track recording is now standard practice; track recording cars and track recording trolleys are built in India.

The first stations of the EIR were not less than 600ft long, and this soon became the minimum platform length permissible on Indian railways. The bigger stations well exceeded this minimum and often the trackwork is arranged so that two trains can be handled independently at one platform face. The longest platforms recently were at Sonepur (2415ft, claimed to be the world's longest). At Kharagpur there is a platform 2350ft long.

Even though more than one footbridge is usually provided at important stations, travellers have a long way to walk and many prefer to take the shortest route across the tracks, even on busy electrified lines. Hence the iron fences which are often built alongside the tracks between the platforms.

The biggest passenger station in India is Calcutta Howrah terminus, rebuilt in 1906 and dealing with both EIR and BNR trains. Calcutta Sealdah terminus is remarkable for its six-mile elevated approach on an embankment, and for its solidity. Its foundations reached 45ft below ground level, and some of its walls are 10ft thick. The 200ft long waiting room was built windowless but had an arcaded clerestory forming an arched gallery. This arrangement, said to be modelled after the palace at Nineveh, provides ventilation while keeping out the rain and the glare. Externally the most grandiose of Indian passenger stations is probably Bombay Victoria terminus (CR). The old GIP Victoria terminus had eight platforms, to which were added five 'main-line' platforms and the spectacular administrative block, built in 1887. Allegedly in the Gothic-Saracenic style, this building was virtually an oriental St Pancras. The rival BBCI never had anything approaching this. In the 1930s it finally built itself a suitable main line terminus at Bombay, some distance from the centre of the city and named Bombay Central, but it was built in the style of its time, its concrete façade suggesting a cinema rather than a railway.

Being built at different periods and places Indian stations offer an abundance of styles. One typical feature is the existence in many towns of both a 'city' station serving the bazaar and commercial centre, and a 'cantonment' station which served the European and administrative area. Also common (as in Russia) has been the building of stations some distance from the town served. This is said to have been intended to isolate the railway from any civil disturbances, and sometimes the British device was adopted of adding 'Road' to the name of the station. For some years after the Mutiny of 1857 it was suggested that all stations serve also as forts. The Government, however, realising that such forts would demand garrisons, never approved this as a general policy. It did recommend that stations in large centres, particularly where there were railway workshops or other key facilities, should indeed be constructed with defence in mind. Thus in 1865 the Public Works Department wrote to the Government of Madras:

> . . . the Government of India considers it would be unwise economy to restrict too closely the cost of protecting these great lines of

communication, by means of which, when completed, the vast territory of the Crown can be held with a diminished military force. The defensive works themselves need not, however, be costly. In general, an enclosure of some kind is demanded for purposes of ordinary security, and an enclosure wall, (with iron gates to close openings) affording no footing on its summit, and flanked by towers or other buildings adapted to give a musketry fire, of which, considering the range of the rifle, there need be very few, and with the exterior cleared of cover for some space around, is all that is really required or contemplated by the Government of India. At the same time, the Government of India did not contemplate in ordinary cases a garrison of troops. It is important, therefore, that the defences should not be disproportionate to the number of employees who can be relied on at such stations . . .

Of the stations whose exteriors leave little doubt of their defensive character, Delhi Junction with its crenellated towers is one good example. Other more benign-looking stations incorporated certain precautions, like those mentioned in the quotation.

Indo-Saracenic motifs were incorporated in many new stations throughout the years of British rule. The new station at Lucknow (1926), built to blend with other public buildings of that provincial capital, was perhaps the most successful and is more pleasing to modern taste than other inter-war stations built in contemporary styles. In recent decades only a few passenger stations have been built or rebuilt, but most of these have proved successful both aesthetically and practically. Even the uncompromising exterior of Ahmedabad station (1966) was compensated by practical conveniences leading to efficiency and cleanliness (helped by a stationmaster who realised that the best way to keep stations clean is to discourage cooking and sleeping on the platforms, and to provide cleaners with brooms which actually sweep).

As stated, the bg was not fully exploited because of restricted clearances. In the nineteenth century and after the maximum width of rolling stock was 10ft 6in, and height 13ft 7in. Although this was later enlarged to 10ft 8in widths on non-suburban, and 12ft on suburban lines, capacity would be significantly increased if these dimensions could be widened further. After all, standard-gauge coaches in the USA are also limited to 10ft 8in. Enlarging Indian coaches to the same gauge/width ratio as in the USA would permit 3 + 3 instead of 3 + 2 seating in chair cars. On the mg better use is made of the track width. In the last century the standard maximum was width 8ft and height 10ft, but 9ft width is now permissible.

SIGNALLING

With so many different railways, and with Government Inspectors insisting on safety as a general requirement rather than on specific systems, the great variety of Indian railways' signalling systems and devices is not surprising. Almost anything which was tried in Britain was tried also in India, and there were also home-made innovations. In the early years revolving discs or signal arms (with separate spectacles) were used, but in line with British practice more sophisticated equipment was soon introduced. The State-operated NWR introduced the indigenous List & Morse interlocking system in 1894, and a year previously Saxby & Farmer (India) had begun to instal cabin interlocking on the GIP Bombay–Delhi line.

The Robertson Report, recording the situation in 1902, mentioned that even on the main lines block instruments did not exist at every station, except on the GIP between Bombay and Jabalpur. On the EIR main line only one-quarter of the stations were thus equipped. On the NWR 45 per cent of stations had interlocking, but only 12 per cent on the GIP and 8 per cent on the BBCI. Some mg lines still allowed two trains to occupy one section by the 'line clear and caution message' system. Robertson additionally complained that some railways treated the distant signal as absolute stop, others as a stop-and-draw-on, and others as a repeater of the home signal. Presumably he had encountered the EIR's modified 'absolute lock and block', which spread to some other lines. In this the block section extended from starter to home signal, rather than from starter to starter. Presumably, too, he had travelled on secondary lines where it was common for outer signals to be placed like distant signals but acting as stop signals.

The lower-quadrant semaphore was typically used, but three-aspect upper-quadrant semaphores existed on some railways. Double-wire signalling, operated by large spoked wheels, was much favoured. Sometimes, however, the two outer signals at a passing station would be operated by a single winch, one wire being wound clockwise and the other anti-clockwise. This made it impossible to pull off both signals at the same time, and was thus an economical form of interlocking. In the inter-war years the token system spread on the more important single-track main lines, replacing the line-clear tickets made out by stationmasters. Many lines adopted Neale's Ball Token; Neale was a GIP engineer and the balls were electrically locked tokens. Lineside pick-up apparatus, illuminated at night by naphtha flares, was installed on many sections. On average in India, block sections were about nine miles long. Signal cabins were rare outside the big junctions; at most block stations there was simply a platform frame.

More modern electrical types of train control were introduced between the World Wars in the Madras, Calcutta and Bombay areas. In the last-named this measure was in connection with electrification. On the BBCI there was automatic signalling and continuous track circuiting between Bombay Churchgate and Virar, with three-aspect colour lights for 38 miles. The new Central Station boasted a 119-lever electro-pneumatic interlocking frame, and an all-electric power frame was installed at Bandra. Electro-mechanical installations and track circuiting exist elsewhere, including some busy mg stations.

Since 1947 there has been considerable investment in modern signalling and communication with the aim of increasing line capacity. Improvements have included multiple-aspect colour-light signals, multiple-aspect upper quadrant semaphores, automatic block, route relay interlocking at busy yards, mechanisation of marshalling yards, track circuiting at stations, a limited introduction of tokenless block, and a beginning with centralised traffic control (CTC). The first installation of CTC was on the NER's congested mg main line between Gorakhpur and Chupra. Colour-light equipment, and much else, was largely imported from Germany, much, however, was made in India sometimes under licence. In the early 1970s an increasing amount of quite complex signalling equipment was being manufactured in India. By 1971 3054 of the 3247 bg block stations were interlocked, 1962 of the 2507 mg, and 16 of the 368 narrow-gauge stations.

FREIGHT AND PASSENGER CARS

Indian railways' freight stock has included all the categories normally encountered in other countries, and a few more besides. In Assam, for example, there was a requirement for jute wagons and for mg elephant wagons. The four-wheel covered wagon was the maid-of-all-work, often carrying freight which in other countries would be loaded in open or hopper wagons. Around the turn of the century the standard box wagon had a six-ton tare and capacity of 12 tons, but by 1910 wagons were being produced of 16 tons capacity by that year all-metal wagons had been standardised. In this period there were also four-wheel open wagons of 8¾ tons tare and 23¼ tons capacity.

By the middle of this century the standard box car had evolved as a 10.5 ton four-wheeler, with a maximum load of 21.5 tons on a 15ft wheelbase. It was of all-metal construction, with buffers and screw couplings. There also existed a heavier variation, of 12 tons tare and 26 tons capacity on a 16ft wheelbase. The mg used a box wagon of 5.5 tons tare, 18 tons capacity and 10ft wheelbase. This also was of metal construction, and in common with all mg stock it had combined centre buffer and coupler.

In the 1970s four-wheel stock such as these box wagons, and the corresponding open, flat, tank and hopper cars remained the most numerous, even though the more important bulk traffics were increasingly being carried in bogie high capacity wagons.

Of the new cars, the BOX type open wagon was the most significant. Designed to carry coal, it has since been used also for other bulk commodities. With a tare of 25 tons, its maximum capacity is 55 tons on its permitted axleload of 20 tons. It has roller bearings, five top-hinged doors on each side, and is suitable for tipping. Designed to run in heavy block trains, it is equipped with centre buffer/couplers.

Other categories of bg bogie freight vehicles also became prominent; the BCX box wagon measures no less than 52ft over couplers, is 12ft 10in high, and 10ft 8in wide. It has two sliding doors on each side, capacity is 54 tons. The buffers and couplers are combined

On the mg also, bogie vehicles have gained an increasing share of traffic. The MBCX box wagon carries a maximum load of 34 tons for a tare weight of 13.4 tons, an axleload of 12 tons, and a length over couplers of 47ft. The corresponding open coal wagon (MBOCX) has a capacity of 35 tons.

The 2ft 6in gauge lines have also maximised their capacity with new bogie vehicles. On an axle load of 8 tons the 37ft open wagon (NOL) can carry 21 tons, as can the NCL box wagon.

Absence of private-owner wagons, stiff demurrage charges and a resolve to buy as few wagons as possible mean that wagon utilisation remains very high compared with railways in most other countries. Although high utilisation is a measure of railway efficency, it can simultaneously mean inefficiency when consignors are delayed by lack of empties. Wagon shortage that is deliberate in the sense that it could be remedied by spending more money on new rolling stock, is chronic. The railways often promise empties to consignors whose traffic seems too valuable to lose. This does not help most railway users. Wagons have been pooled by the several railways since 1919, There were still recently seperate Southern and Northern mg wagon pools.

The vacuum brake was long standard in India, but by the 1960s it seemed to be a major obstacle to the introduction of long trains. Experiments in 1959 with a 6720 ton train hauled by four diesel locomotives over 1 in 60 gradients suggested that regular operation of such trains would require the brakes to be operated from both ends of the train, using either a rear locomotive or a brake van equipped with a vacuum booster. One unique handicap was the flow impedance caused by the grilles fitted to the vacuum pipes to prevent the entry of rats. Indian diesel and electric locomotives are braked by compressed air and need additional equipment to co-ordinate their own brakes with the vacuum brakes of their trains.

Wood, especially Burmese teak, was the favourite material for construction of passenger vehicles until high prices induced some railways to turn to metal. From the early days high standards of comfort were provided in first and second class, but third class passengers were treated austerely. The trouble began right from the very first passenger services, when third class passengers went to the stations in numbers much larger than expected. To accommodate them, overcrowding was accepted, and some third class coaches had their seats removed so as to provide more space.

Probably it was these early difficulties and their solution which established the tradition that third class passengers could be regarded as long-suffering. The EIR and GIPR, however, tried to alleviate the situation in the mid 1860s, with the introduction of 120-seat double-deck four-wheelers for third class passengers. (The Governor of Bombay also travelled in a double-deck four- wheeler. He inhabited the spacious upper-deck bedroom and dining room, while his servants crept around in the bilges). By the turn of the century the more or less standard third class coach was a 27ft long four-wheeler of six compartments. Each compartment contained wooden benches for ten passengers and was separated from the other compartments by vertical iron bars. There were wooden shutters and some variants had glass windows, but there were no lavatories. In 1902 the EIR introduced a new design, which became popular on other railways. This provided longitudinal seats, with upper benches which could be used for baggage or, unofficially, for sleeping. Lavatories were provided. The windows were of glass, and the roof and sides were lined with asbestos.

Main-line trains were usually gas-lit, but there were still many vegetable-oil lamps. A few railways operated a handful of electrically-lit coaches. On average, only half of the Indian railways' passenger stock was fitted with continuous brake, or piped. About 1900 only some lines still provided alarm chains; the other railways had decided that they were ineffectual.

There were some exceptional passenger trains. The GIP was already taking pride in its Bombay–Poona day trains and in 1904 introduced in this service new train sets in which the old sunshades were abandoned in favour of insulated sides, the trains, were moreover vestibuled. They were painted in the new GIP livery : red-brown lower panels and cream uppers. Other Indian railways still used different colours to indicate the class of accommodation.

The BNR's Calcutta–Madras mail train (which also ran over the MSMR) may be taken as an example of the best trains on the eve of World War I. This consisted of eight 68ft bogie vehicles drawn by a 4–4–2 locomotive. From the engine, there was a third/baggage, a third, an inter/third, another inter/third with its two sections separated by a refreshment counter (and no corridor connection), a second/inter/third, a first/second/ servants, a mail and baggage, and a 26 seat restaurant car. The set provided 12 berths for first-class passengers, 24 for second, 79 seats for inter class, seven for passengers' servants, and 286 third-class seats. The third-class coaches featured wooden benches along the sides and back-to-back benches along the centre.

By mid-century the predominating bg designs for the various functions and classes of accommodation were based on a standard 68ft underframe and timber body. The third-class variant of this seated 80 passengers and provided 6 lavatories. Seats were back-to-back, wooden, with four seats on one side of a gangway and one seat on the other side. Two of the lavatories were central, thus dividing the car into two compartments. When one of the latter was intended as a ladies-only section, it was fitted with window bars and internal security catches.

The first class coach provided one six-berth, two twin-berth, and three four berth compartments. As there was no corridor they occupied the full width of the vehicle and each had its own shower and lavatory. A total of 22 berths was available. The lower berths could be raised to form backrests, and the upper berths folded back. Seats were available by day for 33 passengers.

On the mg the general layout was similar, but on a standard 56ft underframe. The third-class coach was divided by an unbroken partition into two sections, each section seating 34 passengers on four-abreast plywood seats. The aisle gangway was along one side with five-abreast seating provided at each end.

In 1955, with Swiss technical assistance, a new coach factory (ICF) was established at Perambur (Madras), initally assembling Swiss-made components. This meant introduction of entirely new coach designs based on a stressed-skin, lightweight, integral design with certain anti-telescoping advantages. With a 70ft body, Schlieren coiled spring bogies, and increased use of plastics, these vehicles offered passengers somewhat higher standards of safety and comfort, while affording a higher passenger/ton ratio.

It is true that first-class passengers had less space than in the older vehicles, but this was in line with the policy of re-designating the former second class as first class. The first class standard coach, unlike its predecessors, included a side corridor, which is why space per passenger was reduced. There were five four-berth compartments and two twin-berth coupés, making a total of 24 berths or 36 seats. The compartments no longer had their own lavatories, but one European-style and three Indian style toilets were installed at the ends of the corridor. One fold-up seat was provided for the coach attendant.

The corresponding third-class coach afforded 80 seats in the conventional arrangement, but only four lavatories; one lavatory per 20 passengers was not altogether agreeable, especially in the early morning when the 70 gal water tanks tended to run dry. Two significant variants based on the standard underframe and shell were the two-tier and three-tier third-class sleeping cars. In the two-tier version there were upholstered upper berths so that in addition to the 80 sitting passengers, 24 sleeping passengers could be carried at night. Equally effective was the three-tier sleeper. In this the middle berths formed backrests during the day, and since there was sleeping accommodation for 75 passengers there was no difference between night and day capacity.

The new coach factory subsequently built integral mg coaches of the same general design. The third-class variant included 64 seats, six doors, and three lavatories. The coach body could withstand a 120 ton compressive load. Legroom (space between seatbacks) was increased from the previous 4ft 10in to the bg standard of 5ft 7in. Hitherto designers seemed to have imagined that passengers on the mg were smaller than on the bg, and that only dwarfs travelled on the narrow gauge.

Although for the purpose of example first and third class cars have been described, many other variants were produced, including several composites. Restaurant cars were interesting in that, as previously, separate vegetarian and non-vegetarian kitchens were provided. Vehicles produced at Perambur at first had blind ends, but were designed so that vestibule gangway connections could be fitted subsequently.

In the 1960s vestibuling was introduced as a general long term policy. First to be converted were bg long-distance coaches, although composites were excluded because of the difficulties involved. On the second and subsequent Rajdhani Expresses it was planned to provide double bellows at the vestibule connection, to counter the dust drawn in at high speeds.

For comparison with the composition of the 1913 Calcutta–Madras mail, detailed above, the 1972 make-up of the mg Delhi–Ahmedabad Express can be considered a typical long-distance fast train: YP Pacific locomotive, baggage car, six third class sitting coaches, two-tier third class sleeper, second, third/RPO composite, first, two third three-tier sleepers, baggage/brake composite, mechanical refrigerator van. Apart from its refrigerator van (a great rarity) this is representative of most long distance services, although in no sense a crack train. Perhaps more indicative of future trends were the Rajdhani expresses described in chapter 3.

STEAM LOCOMOTIVES

In 1965, despite six decades of attempts at standardisation, there were over 80 different classes of bg steam locomotive, 80mg and about 50 on the narrow gauges. Obviously, several volumes would be required to cover the Indian steam locomotive. This section is confined to general trends and standard classes.

Although *Express*, the early EIR locomotive preserved at Jamalpur works, is a 2-2-2T, most early locomotives were of the 2-4-0 and 0-4-2 type. (A GIP 2-4-0 and an NWR 0-4-2 have been preserved). Later, as in Britain, the 0-6-0 freight and 4-4-0 passenger engine became common on both bg and mg. One of the best known types was the mg F series of outside cylinder 0-6-0 built in Scotland and found on several railways. Another interesting design was a bg 4-6-0 built by Dübs for the NWR goods traffic in the 1880s. This type was later adopted by the BNR for its coal trains and, moreover, seems to have served as the basis for the design of the famous Jones Goods locomotive of the Highland Railway in Scotland. One example is preserved at Moghalpura Works in Pakistan.

Partly for the sake of economy, partly in response to military advocacy of standardised locomotives which in time of war could easily be transferred from one railway to another, a standard series of locomotives was designed in 1903, with the help of the British Engineering Standards Association (BESA). These designs had a somewhat higher grate area/ cylinder volume ratio than previous types, in recognition of the replacement of British by Bengal coal, the latter being about 20 per cent inferior in calorific value. Many hundreds of these BESA engines were built, but there was a tendency for the different railways to introduce their own particular modifications, with detail differences. Dimensions of typical BESA types are given in Appendix 2. The BESA bg 4–6–0 was destined to be built until 1951. Its variant on the NWR, type HP, was developed in 1918 to type HPS. The EIR, GIP and MSMR bought their own HPS engines, and in 1925 the EIR introduced a version with a larger boiler, still classified HPS. Because of the failure of the inter-war standard Pacifics, this version was ordered to ease the motive power shortage after World War II. Over 150 serve on Indian Railways; many others went to Pakistan.

Fuel quantity and fuel supply were always, and remained, of more than usual importance in Indian locomotive policy. The BESA engines had been designed on the assumption that the best quality Indian coal would continue to be supplied to the railways, but from about 1914 the price of the higher grades began to rise sharply. Between 1914 and 1922, while bg engine mileage increased by 12 per cent the bg fuel bill more than doubled. Although in the prosperous years after World War I the railways could well afford to pay high prices, prudence demanded engines capable of burning cheaper coal. Since this would entail the use of a wide firebox, the 4–6–2 wheel arrangement was indicated for passenger engines and 2–8–2 for freight.

From 1919 the BBCIR, MSMR and EIR ordered experimental locomotives. The Railway Board refused to sanction all their orders, allowing the BBCIR to obtain only four Pacifics and Mikados (2–8–2s) instead of twenty, and allowing the MSMR to buy two light Pacifics from Baldwin (USA) but refusing permission to buy British Pacifics for direct comparison. Meanwhile, the Locomotive Standards Committee was formed to decide on replacements for the old BESA standards, and track specification were investigated to discover whether heavier engines were feasible. Unfortunately the committee made its recommendations too early to benefit from the lessons provided by the various experimental engines entering service at this time.

For the bg the Locomotive Standards Committee recommended five new IRS ('Indian Railway Standards') designs, to be classified XA, XB, XC (Pacifics), and XD and XE (Mikados). The committee was not concerned with design work, merely recommending general dimensions (which in fact were only loosely followed). The recommended axleloads were 22½ tons for 90lb rail, 19½ tons for 85lb, and 17 tons for 75lb. The adhesion factor (weight on drivers divided by tractive effort) was to be as close as possible to 4.25. The grate area was to be fixed by dividing the tractive effort by 600, and the evaporative and superheating surfaces by multiplying the grate area by 50 and 12 respectively. The revolving parts were to be fully balanced, cylinders to be horizontal, connecting rods short. The existing height restriction was raised from 13ft 6in to 14ft 6in, as it was assumed that BESA engines could be used on lines unable to accommodate the new designs.

With these recommendations from the committee in India, the consulting engineers in London, helped by the British Engineering Standards Association and by the locomotive builders, worked out the designs in detail. Apart from one member of the Locomotive Standards Committee, resident in London, there was little consultation between London and India. In fact the working drawings were never seen in India until after the engines were built. This was quite normal and aroused no comment at the time; consultation would have entailed months of delay.

The first contract was placed in July 1926 with the Vulcan Foundry for 26 XA, 30 XB, and 12 XC units. Other orders followed quickly. The most numerous Pacifics were the XA. with an axle load of only 13 tons. The XB, weighing 90 tons, was somewhat bigger and like the XC was based on the experimental Pacifics previously ordered by the BBCIR. The XC was the largest of the three. On all the engines the rear pair of carrying wheels was mounted on a Cartazzi truck, which had given good service in Britain on the London & North Eastern Pacifics, and Goodall-type drawgear between engine and tender was expected to give the tender more freedom of movement. Some trouble was taken with the bogie design, a representative of the Railway Board visited Swindon to discover why the Great Western Railway preferred spring to gravity control; but in the end the bogie design of the BESA engines was adopted for the Pacifics.

The new Pacifics were used all over India and even the individualistic BNR's 18 M class de Glehn compound Pacifics had the same chassis as the standard XC units. They were allotted the most important duties and soon showed their incapacity to perform them. Despite a modern design of valve gear, with $1\frac{1}{2}$ in steam lap and long travel, steam distribution was poor and caused a sluggish performance, although in this respect the small XA was quite free-running compared to the XB and XC. Steaming quality was likewise poor, and this was especially marked in the XB, which in operation had difficulty in maintaining boiler pressure above 150lb. This was partly due to an incorrect ratio of total tube cross-section to grate area. In the XA and the XC boilers this was a reasonable $11\frac{1}{2}$ per cent, but was only 9 per cent in the XB, which in effect meant that the grate could produce more hot gas than the tubes could pass through the boiler. Even with a full regulator and 33 per cent cut-off these engines were often incapable of accelerating 350-ton trains to 60mph on the level. Availability was low. Up to April 1938 the 284 Pacifics had incurred no fewer than 347 frame fractures and 205 firebox tubeplate cracks. On the BBCIR in 1938 all the engines were temporarily withdrawn because of chronic coupling rod breakages. On the EBR the 18 XB units in 1938 were on average eight years old, and each had spent three of those years in the repair shops.

The growing conviction that these engines were responsible for a number of fatal derailments prompted the Government to take action. The Bihta accident on the EIR in 1937 was the last straw, but in fact ever since their introduction these engines had worried the civil engineering departments of the railways using them. There were at least ten derailments caused by the instability of the XB and XC engines before the Bihta disaster. Moreover, between 1928 and 1937 there were 64 recorded track distortions caused by the 68 XB and XC engines of just one railway.

During the 1930s most railways realised that these locomotives had a pronounced tendancy to oscillate, and took various remedial measures. On some engines the rear truck was set back thirty inches, or the centre of gravity was changed by ballasting, or American drawgear was fitted. But none of these modifications was wholly successful, and speed limits were imposed, varying from 45mph on the NWR to 60mph on the GIPR. For many railways this meant that the engines could no longer be used on mail or express trains and older 4–6–0 engines had to be substituted.

A special investigating committee was despatched from Britain in 1938 at Indian Government request. This included two distinguished locomotive engineers, (Stanier and Cox), and a top-rank civil engineer from the Great Western Railway. After a number of trials the committee made a host of suggestions, including bogie modification, a more rigid drawgear, removal of the Cartazzi slides, frame stiffening, and the fitting of speedometers. It criticised by implication the existing accident inspection standards, and the lack of control over new designs exercised by the Railway Board. Even after modification, the Pacifics remained suspect, and were subject to special speed limits. The whole affair reflected little credit on the railways or on the British locomotive industry. Sundry revelations, and the fact that further orders had been placed even after the engines' instability was well-known, persuaded both houses of the Indian Legislature to censure the Railway Board.

Leading dimensions of the main inter-war locomotive designs are given in Appendix 2. The classes detailed there are not, of course, the only locomotives built during the period. There were a number of experimental designs, and continuations under various type designations of BESA engines, while quite unique designs were ordered by some railways.

Of the latter the BNR was the most prominent, with distinctive passenger engines, and Garratts for its coal traffic. The Garratt concept was also used expertimentally by the NWR, which tested it against the Mallet, and apparently was impressed by neither, continuing to use pairs of 2–8–os for its most steeply graded lines. The mg Assam Bengal Railway was also using Garratts in Assam in the 1940s, although its Assam Mail of 24 bogie vehicles was usually entrusted to a pair of standard Mikados.

In 1940 the Indian Railways possessed 5347 bg, 2320 mg and 302 narrow-gauge locomotives. The biggest stock was held by the EIR with 1529 (bg only) units, followed by the NWR with 1186 bg and 100 narrow and the BNR with 743 bg and 116 narrow-gauge. The largest mg locomotive fleets were those of the BBCIR which had 490 units, besides 373 bg and 25 narrow, and the SIR with 401 mg, 152 bg and 11 narrow-gauge engines.

After World War II the locomotive stock was badly run down and insufficient for the demands made on it, despite delivery in the 1940s of over 1000 units from Canada and the USA. The most useful of these acquisitions were the standard wartime 2–8–2 engines of class AWD (from the USA) and CWD (from Canada) which greatly relieved the locomotive shortage. The standard US Transportation Corps 2–8–0 appeared (AWC), and also a heavy 2–8–2 (AWE) both on the bg. On the mg about 300 units of US 2–8–2s (MAWD) were acquired and proved very useful, despite a speed restriction imposed to prevent their bogie tenders leaving the track.

By the mid-1950s the locomotive situation was being transformed by the acquisition of hundreds of Pacifics and Mikados of the new WP and WG designs. The WP was designed in the mid-1940s, and 16 prototypes (WP/P) were obtained from Baldwin in 1947-49. Lessons from an experimental pre-war

Pacific were incorporated in the design, which was, however, quite new. For a mail and express engine, the 5ft 7in driving wheels seemed somewhat small, but in practice this proved no handicap and the small diameter did make space for the deep firebox essential to provide sufficent steam without the use of a mechanical stoker. The WP had bar frames, and proved to be a steady engine. Its boiler was slightly superior to that of the somewhat larger XC. With coal of 12,500 BTU/lb, both boilers, consuming 3200 lb/hr, could evaporate 28,000 lb/hr. The XC's bigger boiler was compensated by the WP's larger superheater (683 sq ft against 636). With its higher boiler pressure and improved steam distribution the WP was regarded as 10 per cent more efficient than the XC.

The WG 2–8–2, a mixed-traffic engine intended primarily for freight haulage, used the same boiler as the WP, but its design was more in the British tradition. Its specification will be found in Appendix 2. It appeared in 1950, the first 100 units being built in Britain. As with the WP, it was later supplied by a variety of builders, Canada, USA, Britain, Poland, Austria, France, Germany, Italy, Japan, not to speak of India herself, built one or both of these basic types, many units being financed by the Colombo Plan. The two last designs to be built for Indian Railways were the WT 2–8–4T, originally intended for Calcutta commuter traffic, and a light Pacific with the same boiler, class WL. The latter originated with ten engines supplied by Vulcan in 1955. A decade later another 94 units were built in India to replace some of the older 4–6–0 types. By 1972 many Eastern Railway engines, mainly WP and WG, were fitted with the Giesl Ejector. The Central Railway was also experimenting with this device on six WP Pacifics, but was having clogging difficulties.

The most useful mg engine at the end of World War II was still the BESA 4–6–0, which had been built in several detail variations and under several type classifications. However, between the wars new 4–6–2 (classes YB and YC) and 2–8–2 (YD) types had taken over the heaviest duties, while on the secondary lines had appeared the YF 0–6–2 and its derivative the YF/M 2–6–2, besides the YK 2–6–0. The post-war mg designs corresponding to the bg WP and WG were the YP Pacific and YG Mikado. The YP prototypes arrived from Baldwin in 1949, and incorporated many of the features of the WP (bar frames, thermic syphon, deep firebox). The YG, for freight, used the same boiler, and was of very similar appearance. Like their WP and WG contemporaries, they were built in large numbers by various countries, although the domestic private builder Telco (a Tata company) predominated. For lighter duties, 2–6–2 prototypes of class YL were built in Britain in 1953, to be followed by production units from Germany, Hungary and Japan.

For the 2ft 6in gauge lines six IRS standard designs had been worked out in the 1920s, but only two were built on a large scale. These were the ZB 2–6–2 and the ZE 2–8–2. Both had 2ft 10in driving wheels, but the ZB had a 6 ton axleload against the 8 tons of the ZE. They were derived, respectively, from existing NWR and BNR designs. After 1947 ZB and ZE units were obtained from a variety of builders. From time to time other designs appeared, but only in small numbers. Most narrow-gauge lines relied heavily on old non-standard engines.

Steam locomotive ownership reached a peak in 1964 with 10,810 units. It then slowly declined, reaching 9,387 in 1971.

ELECTRIC AND DIESEL TRACTION

From the mid-1950s, dieselisation and electrification were pushed ahead, with the main aim of increasing line capacity on heavily trafficked sections. In retrospect it is hard to see how the steam locomotive could have coped efficiently with the ever-increasing bulk traffic originating in Eastern India. Yet controversy over the respective merits of the different forms of traction has shown no sign of abating. Among rail-waymen, argument has been more muted than in the public press. It was possible however, to obtain, in private, very penetrating critiques of dieselisation policy from engineers engaged in electrification, while diesel engineers could produce shrewd arguments against electrification. The points raised by these experts were often quite different from those mentioned in the press.

Opponents of electrification claimed that cost studies produced to show the economic advantage of electric locomotives over steam were based on steam engine costs which were combined main line and shunting averages, whereas the electric locomotive costs were for main-line operation only, with their more efficient utilisation of inputs. (Moreover, in practice steam shunting continued on electrified lines, as did steam operation of certain passenger and slow freight trains; electric locomotives were too scarce and costly to waste on such services). It was alleged that in cost calculations the high cost of diesel fuel was not offset by subtracting the import duty component, which after all went to the government. Moreover, the possibility of replacing imported oil by coke derivatives was ignored. The alleged high cost of maintenance of electric equipment was played down, although the daily thefts of catenary wire, which certainly did reduce the value of electrification, could not of course have been foreseen. Controversialists suffering from war psychosis resulting from India's military conflicts argued that catenary was very vulnerable to air attack (an argument duly refuted by reference to Germany during World War II). It was said that the electrification decisions of the mid-1950s were the result of political pressure on behalf of Bombay, Calcutta and Madras, and against the advice of railway mechanical engineers.

The advocates of electrification maintain that in any case the steam locomotive consume too much high-grade coal. Although India has great coal resources, the production of the higher grades has not been sufficient to satisfy both the railways' growing demands and the needs of the new metallurgical industry. In fact, new coal washing plants have allowed somewhat lower grades of coal to be used by the railways. In addition, the transport of locomotive coal is a problem in itself, pre-empting valuable line and train capacities. It seems impossible moreover to stop large-scale pilferage of locomotive coal. Electric locomotives consume, through the medium of power stations, only the lowest grades of coal. Dieselisation is not a good answer because India produces little oil. Not only is oil fuel a drain on precious foreign currency reserves, but it is subject to international circumstances and vulnerable in wartime. Whilst the chemical and road transport industries and defence and modern farming activities have no alternatives to oil, the railways have, and should therefore use them. Diesel locomotives have a working life only about one-third that of electric traction equipment, diesel replacement components are expensive, and so is diesel maintenance. High diesel maintenance costs, it is alleged, are camouflaged by presenting combined diesel and steam maintenance expenditure in official statistics. For reasons such as these the critics of dieselisation hold that diesel traction must be regarded only as an interim measure on lines which are too heavily trafficked to be worked by steam, but have not yet been electrified.

How the respective 'spheres of influence' of the electrifiers and the dieselisers would be allotted was still a controversial matter by the early 1970s. But it is not really an urgent problem. Both electrification and dieselisation are needed to keep the traffic moving and neither has yet been overdone. There are lines whose high traffic densities plainly justify electrification, and many of these cannot be electrified in the next decade or so. Therefore diesels are genuinely needed.

India's first electric trains started running in 1925, on a length of the GIP's suburban mileage out of Bombay. In the inter-war years this system expanded over the Thull Ghat as far as Igatpuri on the GIP main line to the North and East and over the Bhore Ghat to Poona, significantly easing the working of these two heavily graded main lines, which had hitherto required the assistance of heavy tank locomotives. There was additional suburban electrification in Bombay, not only by the GIP but also by the BBCI to Virar. In Madras, too, there was a suburban electrification on the SI mg line to Tambaram. In 1947 there were 223 route miles of bg electrification, and 18 miles of mg. All were on the 1500V dc

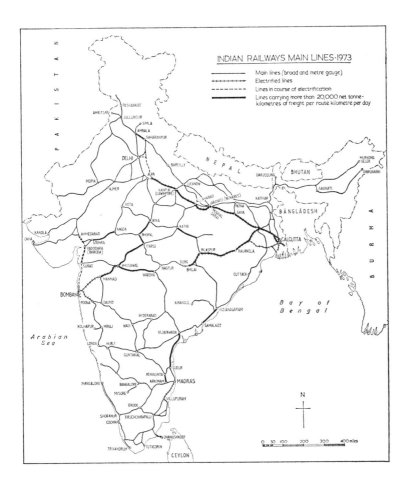

INDIAN RAILWAYS MAIN LINES·1973

Main lines (broad and metre gauge)
Electrified lines
Lines in course of electrification
Lines carrying more than 20,000 net tonne-
kilometres of freight per route kilometre per day

system. In 1958, to alleviate overcrowding, two suburban sections were electrified at Calcutta at 3000V dc. It had already been decided in 1957, however, to adopt for future projects the 25kV single-phase ac system. The Calcutta and Madras lines were subsequently converted to this system, but the Bombay lines remained unchanged.

The first post-war main-line electrifications were of heavy traffic routes on the ER and SER, especially of lines serving the new metallurgical projects in West Bengal and Bihar. The line with the heaviest traffic, from Durgapur to Moghal Sarai, which was already operated by imported diesels, was included. By 1961 bg electrified mileage had grown to 446 miles. Later, more Eastern coalfield routes were electrified, and additional suburban lines in Calcutta, beginning with those from Sealdah. Existing electrifications were extended.

By 1971 there were 2200 miles of bg electrification, and 103 miles of mg (Madras). This mileage included an extension (at 25kV) of the GIP electrification, from Igatpuri to Bhusaval, and of the Madras scheme from Tambaram to Villupuram. Electrification of the key main line from Moghal Sarai to Delhi was under way and was completed as far as Tundla (near Agra) in 1972. The SER electrification towards Nagpur was complete as far as Durg. Work was in progress on the former BBCI main line from Bombay to Ahmedabad; it was expected that this route would be electrified by 1974. Because the initial section to Virar is already electrified at 1500V, dual-voltage locomotives are to be used. Approval has also been given for converting the Madras–Vijayawada section of the Madras–Calcutta line. Thus the future pattern of electrification seems clear. Three bg main lines would initially be electrified: Howrah–Delhi, Howrah–Bombay via Nagpur, and Bombay–Ahmedabad. Later possiblities were Bombay–Delhi and Madras–Calcutta.

India's first electric locomotives, supplied from Britain in the 1920s, were still at work in the 1970s. The first post-war locomotives were also British-built, but in 1962 the first Indian-built electric appeared. This was a standard WCM type

360hp unit for the Central Railway's dc lines, and incorporated British components, including English Electric traction equipment. Two years later India produced her first ac electric, a WAG1 type unit of a BB series designed by a European consortium which included the major French concern Alsthom. Apart from British imports and technical help with the dc units, and West European with the ac locomotives, Indian Railways also imported units from Japan. But by the early 1970s they were able to design and put into production their own locomotives. In 1971 more powerful units for both the dc and ac lines were designed, while work was in progress on a dual-voltage locomotive for the WR. In 1970–71, 50 electric locomotives were built in India, and none were imported. The total electric locomotive stock in 1971 was 582 bg and 20 mg. The output of locomotives hardly kept pace with demand, and on some electrified sections passenger trains continued to be steam hauled.

Diesel locomotives in 1971 totalled 872 bg, 264 mg, and 33 narrow gauge. About 700 were of the WDM2 type, an Alco 2600 hp Co-Co bg design which was chosen for home production. Other types included several General Motors designs, and a small batch of British diesel-hydraulics which had been introduced (with scant success) on an arid mg section of the Western Railway in the earliest days of dieselisation. The WDS3 was a MAK diesel-hydraulic shunter, fitted with the Indian-designed Suri transmission. The WDS4 was a 660hp shunting and branch line diesel-hydraulic unit of MAK design which was adopted for series production at Chitaranjan Works. Other diesel-hydraulics included the Henschel WDM3, a 2500hp BB unit with 19 ton axleload. On the mg, the YDM4, another Alco design, was the standard main line unit. For the narrow gauge a powerful (20hp per ton) 700hp design was built by MAK and Chitaranjan for the Kalka–Simla and Nagpur area lines (ZDM type). Diesel railcars were never in very widespread use in India, but a prototype was built by the ICF at Perambur in the 1960s and was followed by ten production units for the SR and NER mg lines; These were for first and second class passengers only. More are expected to follow.

By 1972 70 per cent of freight tonne-km were produced by diesel or electric traction. The percentage of trains hauled by electric or diesel locomotives would have been considerably less than this, because diesels and electrics were allocated to the fastest, heaviest and longest-distance trains; that is, to those trains which produced the best operating statistics. Ousting steam traction from the most productive runs meant that, statistically speaking, steam increasingly bore the burden of the inherently inefficient short-distance, low-traffic, and infrequent services.

As elsewhere, this meant that steam traction efficiency indices declined, and by 1972 the deterioration of steam loco-motives operating statistics already more than offset the savings attributable to the dieselised services. In other words, in economic, as distinct from operational terms, further dieselisation was likely to be disadvantageous. That is another way of saying that some operations were cheaper with steam than with diesel traction.

Railways in other countries have encountered the same problem, even though they rarely admit it. This is especially relevant in India because of the large proportion of branch and secondary services, which neither lend themselves to high-intensity operation nor to abandonment. Further diesel-isation, however, is required to ease traffic flows, and this must eventually reduce the steam locomotive stock to a few hundred scattered units engaged on unproductive work; at which point it would be economically advantageous to elimin-ate the steam infrastructure entirely.

Recently some thought at last was being given to the best utilisation of the steam locomotive in its last decades. Diesel-isation hitherto has been of trains rather than areas, which means that an underemployed steam infrastructure is main-tained in diesel territory (and to a lesser extent in electrified areas). The closure of some of these depots and works, and the concentration of steam traction in particular areas, is likely, but recently at least no firm desision had been taken.

SELF SUFFICIENCY

At independence, in 1947, the Indian railways were importing about one-third of their equipment and stores. This was progressively reduced to about 5 per cent in 1970. The aim was to reserve scarce foreign currency for unavoidable expenditure, and to reduce dependence on outside sources. The usual procedure was to obtain the assistance of foreign suppliers in setting up production in India, sometimes by providing technical assistance, sometimes by establishing Indian subsidiaries. The State-owned factories producing large items meanwhile encouraged smaller industries to supply components.

Although under British rule most locomotives were built in Britain, between 1885 and 1923 214 bg locomotives were built at the EIR Jamalpur works, while from 1896 to 1940 the Ajmer works of the BBCIR built 435 mg engines. The advantages of domestic construction included closer co-operation between builders and users, and, in theory, lower costs. The cost advantage hardly materialised, but the existence of locomotive building capacity in India no doubt induced British suppliers to keep their prices down. In 1921, with Government of India encouragement, the Peninsular Locomotive Company was formed to build locomotives in its new works at Jamshedpur. However, a reduced demand for locomotives, plus the failure to obtain tariff protection, caused this enterprise to fail before producing a single engine. In 1947 Ajmer was producing some bg 0–4–2T engines, but ceased production in 1950, by which time the new works at Chittaranjan in the Eastern industrial area was ready. Chittaranjan was India's foremost production unit in the State-owned sector of the economy. With help from British locomotive builders it produced its first engine, a WG 2–8–2, in 1950. Early in 1972 it built its last steam engine, a YG 2–8–2, making a total production of 1908 WG, 259 WP, 30 WT, 94 WL and 60 YG units before it turned over entirely to main-line electric and diesel shunting locomotive manufacture. Most metre gauge YP and YG engines were built by a private company (Tata), initially with German assistance.

The second manufacturing unit of Indian Railways was the Integral Coach Factory at Perambur (Madras). ICF began production in 1955 and in its first 16 years built over 8000 passenger traffic vehicles, including mu stock. Claimed to be the largest railway coach building factory in the world, its output was supplemented by two other State enterprises, Hindustani Aircraft and Bharat Earthmovers, and one private company, Jessop. Wagons were constructed mainly by private builders, who frequently complained that they could have built more wagons at a lower price if the Ministry of Railways had been less disorganised in its placing of orders.

The third manufacturing unit administered by Indian Railways was the Diesel Locomotive Works, which started production at Benares (Varanasi) in 1964. The DLW enjoyed the cooperation of Alco and US financial assistance. The offer of a diesel locomotive works on attractive terms was no doubt influential in formulating dieselisation policy. Opponents of dieselisation have argued that the main beneficiary of the deal was Alco rather than Indian Railways. However, apart from providing Indian built diesel locomotives, the DLW also introduced useful high-precision manufacturing techniques to India. Output was 68 units in 1970–71, against an eventual planned annual output of 150. By that year about four-fifths by value of a completed diesel locomotive consisted of Indian-produced components. Traction motors for both diesel and electric locomotives came from another State enterprise, Heavy Electricals of Bhopal.

Technical research, and its incorporation into new designs of locomotives, rolling stock, and structures was the responsibility of the Research, Designs & Standards Organisation (RDSO). This body, with its headquarters in Lucknow, was formed in 1957 from the amalgamation of the Central Standards Office and the Railway Testing & Research Centre. Apart from designing railway equipment, it had responsibilities for standard setting and inspection. As a consultant organisation it also began to offer technical advice to other Asian railway systems. Not unconnected with this was the emergence of India as an exporter of railway equipment. Most has been designed for Asia, ICF has exported passenger vehicles to Taiwan and Jessop to Burma. Freight wagons, however, have been delivered to Yugoslavia, springs to Poland, and couplings even to Western Germany. Users of steam locomotives in other countries have been offered spare parts which were becoming unobtainable elsewhere. Exports were still small in the early 1970s, but they emphasise that, for India, railways have a future as well as a past.

Appendices

APPENDIX 1

THE FOREIGN TRAVELLER IN INDIA

THE day has gone when the European could expect to be pampered on Indian railways. The obsequious railway servant has almost disappeared, to be replaced by men who, on average, are probably more painstaking than their European counterparts. Any special consideration the foreign traveller receives will be because he is, after all, a visitor, whilst a first-class ticket still commands respect. The intending visitor to India should not be deterred by any of the unpleasantnesses described elsewhere in this book; he is very unlikely indeed to suffer, or even see, violence. This is probably true even of the Eastern Railway, because at the time of writing the political situation in Bengal seems to be stabilised. Travellers on the ER, however, (and others), may reasonably expect some of their trains to be delayed by chain-pullers and, if they travel first class, occasionally to share their compartment with crowds of polite but inconvenient students.

Contrary to popular belief, Europeans are not prevented from travelling third class. Since fares are so low, however, the extra comfort and security of air-conditioned or first-class travel is well worthwhile. The foreign visitor has so many physical problems that there is little point in adding to them by travelling in the lower classes. First-class compartments can be, and at night should be, locked from the inside. The windows are protected by four lines of defence: glass, gauze, and louvred shutters, plus fixed iron bars. The traveller may be confronted by various notices, which are usually worth heeding: 'Less baggage, more comfort'; 'Cleanliness is next to godliness'; 'Beware of thieves asking for permission to sleep on the floor of this carriage. Please don't accept food, drink, or tobacco from strangers, These may be doped . . .' 'East or west, train is best'.

First-class berths are upholstered and covered with Rexine-type material. Bedding is not provided, although between large stations bed rolls can be hired, as can loaded ice boxes. First-class reservations are difficult to obtain at short notice although, as with the other classes, most demand is for the best trains. It is almost always possible to obtain reservations on long-distance stopping trains. This means that a traveller who has not made advance bookings should allow generous margins in his schedule. In any case, India is not the place for people in a hurry.

Reservations are applied for in writing, usually on forms provided by the reservations offices. Tickets have to be purchased concurrently. Details of reservation procedures, fare tables, and other information for travellers is exhaustively presented in the timetables. The official *All-India Railway Timetable* is published in English by the Railway Board, while a private company publishes *Newman's Indian Bradshaw*. One or other of these is usually obtainable from station bookstores. The first has fewer misprints than *Indian Bradshaw*, is closer to the horse's mouth, and provides a map, but *Bradshaw* additionally gives information on air services, and rail services in Pakistan, Bangladesh, and Ceylon. Indian Government tourist offices abroad distribute a condensed railway timetable, detailing the best trains between important points.

The warnings given by most guidebooks about food and drink should be carefully heeded. Station restaurants, which tend to be dingy but leisurely, can provide suitable sustenance for Europeans (that is, food and drink which has been thoroughly cooked). Tea and coffee, boiled eggs, porridge, and rice are likely to be the mainstay of railway travellers intent on escaping the horrors of digestive ailments. Shops stock few items of manufactured foods, although tinned biscuits, cornflakes, and powdered milk are usually obtainable. Outside the larger towns, hotels may be unprepossessing or non-existent. Railway retiring rooms, providing bed and bathroom, are cheap and usually clean and have the advantage of being situated at the larger stations. They are obtained on a first-come, first-served basis, and tend to be fully occupied at the places where hotels are least adequate. Problems of travel and accommodation can often be solved with the help of the Government tourist offices located in a few foreign cities and all over India. Guidebooks are almost essential. Among other things they indicate the best time of year to visit the different regions. Because tourist attractions and items of railway interest are distributed so widely, it is possible, and well worthwhile, to combine both pursuits. The new Railway Museum in Delhi might be a good place to start.

APPENDIX 2

REPRESENTATIVE STEAM LOCOMOTIVES

Class	Type	Cylinders (two) in.	Driving Wheels	Boiler Pressure lb/sq in.	Grate Area (sq ft)	Tractive Effort (lb)	Axleload (tons)	Year of Introduction	Total Units in Service in 1965* (excluding Pakistan)
APC	Broad gauge BESA	20¼ × 26	6ft 6in	180	32	21,432	17·7	1908	11
BTC	Broad gauge BESA	20 × 26	5ft 1½in	180	25·3	25,873	17·4	1907	42
HPS	Broad gauge BESA	20¼ × 26	6ft 2in	180	32	22,591	18·0	1915	152
SGC	Broad gauge BESA	20 × 26	5ft 1½in	180	25·3	25,873	17·4	1905	366
SGS	Broad gauge BESA	20 × 26	5ft 1½in	180	25·3	25,873	16·8	1909	91
SPS	Broad gauge BESA	20 × 26	6ft 2in	180	25·3	21,503	17·0	1905	47
HGS	Broad gauge BESA	22 × 26	4ft 8½in	180	32	34,077	16·2	1902	135
PS	Metre/gauge BESA	16½ × 22	4ft 9in	180	15·4	16,077	9·4	1905	70
XA	Broad gauge IRS	18 × 26	5ft 1½in	180	32	20,960	13·1	1929	95
XB	Broad gauge IRS	21¼ × 28	6ft 2in	180	45	26,760	17·1	1923	62
XC	Broad gauge IRS	23 × 28	6ft 2in	180	51	30,625	19·8	1928	49
XD	Broad gauge IRS	22¼ × 28	5ft 1½in	180	45	35,260	17·2	1925	194
XE	Broad gauge IRS	23½ × 30	5ft 1½in	180	60	48,086	22·5	1929	93
XT	Broad gauge IRS	12 × 22	4ft 3in	210	14	11,088	14·9	1930	77
YB	Metre gauge IRS	16 × 24	4ft 9in	180	23	16,492	9·7	1928	140
YD	Metre gauge IRS	17 × 24	4ft 0in	180	26	22,110	9·9	1928	153
YF	Metre gauge IRS	14 × 22	4ft 5in	160	17·75	13,638	8·1	1929	80
CWD, AWD	Broad gauge US	21 × 28	5ft 0in	200	47	35,000	16·1	1944	708
MAWD	Metre gauge US	16 × 24	4ft 0in	185	27·6	20,128	8·9	1942	304
WM	Broad gauge Standard	16 × 28	5ft 7in	210	24·6	19,043	16·2	1940	70
WP	Broad gauge Standard	20¼ × 28	5ft 7in	210	46	30,600	18·6	1947	536*
WG	Broad gauge Standard	21¾ × 28	5ft 1½in	210	46	38,890	18·5	1950	2,102*
WL	Broad gauge Standard	19¼ × 28	5ft 7in	210	38	27,640	16·9	1955	10*
WT	Broad gauge Standard	20¼ × 28	5ft 7in	210	38	30,600	18·0	1959	10*
YG	Metre gauge Standard	16½ × 24	4ft 0in	210	28	23,450	10·5	1950	1,004*
YP	Metre gauge Standard	15¼ × 24	4ft 6in	210	28	18,400	10·5	1950	563*
YL	Metre gauge Standard	12¼ × 22	3ft 7in	210	17·75	13,700	8·1	1953	264
ZB	2ft 6in gauge IRS	12 × 18	2ft 10in	160	14	10,368	6·0	1928	43
ZE	2ft 6in gauge IRS	16 × 18	2ft 10in	160	22·2	18,432	8·0	1927	61

*Post-war designs were built up to 1972, by which time their totals were: WG 2450; WP 755; WL 104; WT 30; YG 1074; YP 871.

APPENDIX 3

ZONAL RAILWAY MAPS

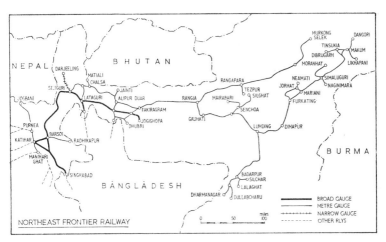

NORTHEAST FRONTIER RAILWAY

▬▬▬	BROAD GAUGE
─────	METRE GAUGE
++++++	NARROW GAUGE
-------	OTHER RLYS

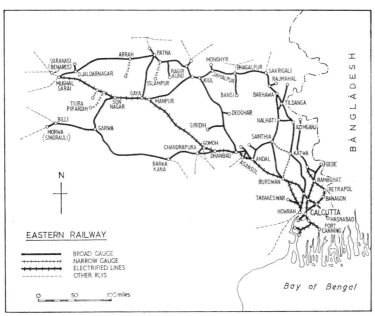

EASTERN RAILWAY

▬▬▬	BROAD GAUGE
++++++	NARROW GAUGE
━━━━	ELECTRIFIED LINES
-------	OTHER RLYS

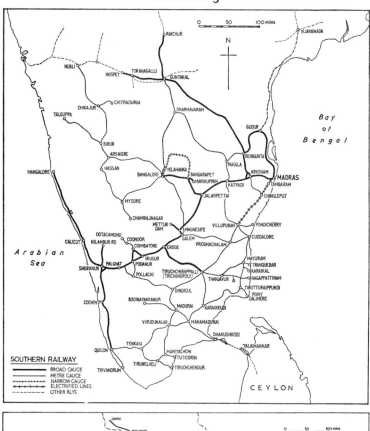

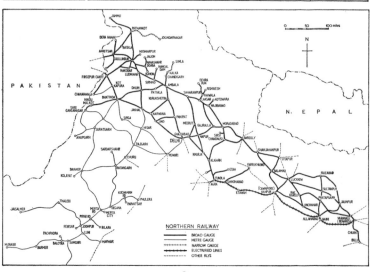

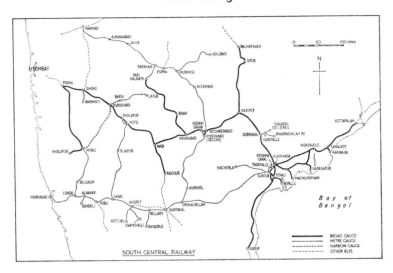

SOUTH CENTRAL RAILWAY

APPENDIX 3

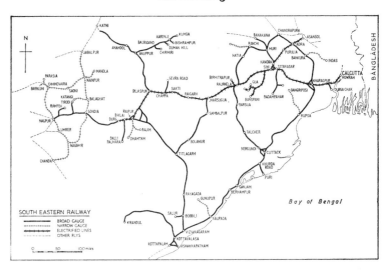

APPENDIX 3

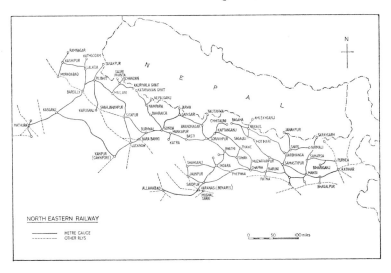

NORTH EASTERN RAILWAY

——————— METRE GAUGE
- - - - - - - OTHER RLYS

Bibliography

ALTHOUGH much official and semi-official material has been published about Indian railways, this is nowadays not always easy to find, and there has been little attempt in this century to use this material to produce a general history of the railways in India. The researcher is probably best located in England or India, because USA libraries were always more interested in acquiring Japanese and Chinese material and tended to ignore India. In Britain the library of the former India Office, the British Museum Reading Room, and India House have useful collections.

A basic source is the Railway Board's *History of Indian Railways Constructed and in Progress*. This, published from time to time in updated editions, gives a short introductory history and then treats each railway in turn, providing dates of opening for the different sections, track details, gradients, and financial matters. Other useful official publications are various *Technical Reports, Railway Accident Reports, Annual Reports* as well as occasional papers such as the *Railway Corruption Enquiry Committee Report* (1955), the Indian Railway Enquiry Committees' reports of 1937 and 1947, the Robertson and Acworth reports, *Fuel Economy on Indian Railways* (1954), and *Millions on the Move* (1948). This last is an account of the post-Partition (1947) refugee traffic.

The former railway companies also published their annual reports as well as their rates and regulations. An example of the latter is the Great Indian Peninsula Railway's occasional *Information as to Rates and Fares*, which informs its readers, among other things, that the fare for tiger cubs travelling by passenger train is double the dog fare. Another informative book is *The Indian Rail-*

way Servant's Manual by J. Hardless (Calcutta, 1898) in which operating procedures, railwaymen's duties, and such facts that railwaymen retired at 55, are to be found arranged in alphabetical order. Information on the early railway proposals and the problem of finding capital is conveyed by L. Jenks, *Migration of British Capital to 1875* (New York, 1927), and D. Thorner, *Investment in Empire* (Philadelphia 1950). The section on railway thieves is derived from Paparau Nayuda's *History of Railway Thieves* (Madras 1915).

Over the years there have been many studies of Indian railways from the economic and commercial point of view, often written by academics. The following are a selection:

K. Aiyar, *Indian Railways* (Oxford, 1925)

J. Johnson, *Economics of Indian Rail Transport* (Bombay, 1960)

A. Prasad, *Indian Railways* (Bombay, 1960)

V. Ramanadham, *Indian Railway Finance* (Delhi, 1956)

N. Sanyal, *Development of Indian Railways* (Calcutta, 1930)

K. Saxena, *Indian Railways* (Bombay, 1962)

S. Srivastava, *Transport Development in India* (Ghaziabad, 1956)

R. Tivari, *Railways in Modern India* (Bombay, 1941)

G. Khosta's *Railway Management in India* was due recently for publication. In 19th-century Britain much pamphleteering was devoted to the advocacy or the condemnation of this or that railway scheme, while at the same time a few authors tried to produce books of a more lasting value. Three of the latter are: H. Bell, *Railway Policy in India* (London, 1894); E. Davidson, *The Railways of India* (London, 1868); and H. Trevor, *Railways in British India* (London, 1891). Bell's work concentrates on standards and policies, while Davidson gives a good deal of informaton on the engineering of the early railways.

Other engineering information is contained in A. Addis's *Hints to Young Engineers employed on Indian Railways* (London, 1910). For a history of one railway company, written by a former manager, there is G. Huddleston's *History of the East Indian Railway* (Vol. 1: Calcutta 1906; Vol. 2: Bristol 1939). Nothing comparable seems to exist about the other railway companies. B. de Villeroi's *History of the North Western Railway* (Lahore, 1896) is little more than a polemic. However, the NWR receives good coverage in several of its aspects from two of its former servants: V. Bayley, *Permanent Way through the Khyber* (London, 1934), and P. S. Berridge, *Couplings to the Khyber* (Newton Abbot, 1969). The Bengal Nagpur Railway is the background of two volumes of Indian reminiscences by former British officials: J. Mitchell, *Wheels of Ind* (London, 1934); and P. Napier, *Raj in Sunset* (Ilfracombe, 1961). There is not much readily available material on rolling stock and equipment. For locomotives, there is a collection of photographs with textual accompaniment in M. Harrison's *Indian Locomotives of Yesterday. Part 1. Broad Gauge* (Bracknell, 1972), a kind of do-it-yourself booklet in which the author has left blank spaces in those sections for which information was not easily available. The Pacific locomotive misfortune gets authoritative airing in the *Report by Sir J. Thom on the cause of the railway accident near Bihta on 17 July 1937* (Delhi, 1938); and *Pacific Locomotive Committee 1938–39; Report* (Delhi 1939).

J. C. Mackay's *Light Railways for the United Kingdom, India and the Colonies* (London, 1896) has some technical information on the earlier metre and narrow gauge lines. The narrow gauge lines, and especially their locomotives, are detailed in *Indian Narrow Gauge Railways* (Richmond, 1969) by H. Hughes and F. Jux; this is a book which resembles its subject, packing much material within a small compass. A similar study of the mg by Hughes was awaited recently.

Back issues of *The Railway Gazette* and the *Locomotive, Carriage & Wagon Review* frequently contain illustrated articles on Indian locomotives

To some extent the lack of general books about Indian railways, their history and equipment, is filled by two volumes celebrating respectively the centenaries of Indian and Pakistani railways: J. Sahni, *Indian Railways 1853–1953* (Delhi, 1953); and M. Malik, *Hundred Years of Pakistani Railways* (Karachi, 1962).

Railway periodicals also provide useful information. The *Railway Magazine* and *Railway World* have published occasional first-hand accounts of one or another aspect, while *The Railway Gazette* and *Modern Railways*, both published in Britain, transmit current information, usually derived from official sources. In the past *The Railway Gazette* has published very useful special Indian issues, notably those of 17 September, 1923, 11 November and 2 December, 1929. The Railway Ministry publishes its monthly *Indian Railways*, for which the overseas subscription was recently only

£0.90 or US$2.20. Finally, there are two excellent novels in a railway setting. The first is set among railwaymen in the last years of British rule, while the second recalls the horrors of the refugee trains of 1947. Both are published in several editions: *Bhowani Junction*, by John Masters, and *Train to Freedom*, by Kushwant Singh.

Index

Note : The current official spelling of place-names is shown in parentheses, the 1972 railway timetable being used as source. Index compiled by J. van den Broeke.